Hitler Youth: the duped generation

H W Koch

Editor-in-Chief: Barrie Pitt
Editor: David Mason
Art Director: Sarah Kingham
Picture Editor: Robert Hunt
Consultant Art Editor: Denis Piper
Designer: David A Evans
Illustration: John Batchelor
Photographic Research: Jonathan Moore
Cartographer: Richard Natkiel

Contents

Search for a better Germany

Introduction by S.L. Mayer

Those who maintain an interest in the Third Reich, particularly young people who were born during or after the Second World War, are forced to ask themselves the same question: How could millions of young Germans have followed Hitler? This question cannot ever be fully answered, and the usual feeling is that Nazis, and especially young people who were drawn to Nazism, were either perverted, racist, misled or perhaps a combination of all of these. Yet millions of young people, both voluntarily and in-

voluntarily, joined the Hitler Youth and, fought for it during the war. And this is the bit that sticks in the craw: they were enthusiastic about it too.

It would be puerile and ahistorical to conclude that all these millions of young people were twisted and warped by a propaganda machine which relentlessly raised them through the schools and into the army. There are many naive and easily malleable people in the world and in Germany; and yet, could they *all* have been so naive, so malleable that they could ignore the sinister character and evil inherent in the Third Reich? In 1939 there were over eight million members of the Hitlerjugend, between the ages of ten and eighteen. Religion has always been a powerful ideological feature of German homes. How could these young people reconcile Christianity with Nazism?

H W Koch provides many of the answers to these questions. He shows that the yearning for a compromise between an increasingly ugly, industrialized Germany on the one hand and the exquisite, hauntingly beautiful German countryside on the other led many people of various religious and social origins to work for a régime which promised, and delivered, full employment as well as a synthesis between a modern industrial society and the volkish, time-honored traditions of the German past. The New Order promised national renewal, a revival of national pride, and national unity of all groups in the face of national humiliation brought on by defeat in the First World War and the vague, and largely unfulfilled democratic ideals of the Weimar Republic.

The German youth movement was popular before 1933. Like German industry and politics, the youth movements of the prewar period and the twenties were subject to the *Gleichschaltung* of 1933 and after. They too were to be united and reorganized into one body to serve both German youth and the state. A healthy body and a healthy mind were Athenian ideals which Hitler promised to revive in the Hitlerjugend. The massive organization constructed under Baldur von Schirach won genuine support among the young people of Germany, many of whom rejected the bourgeois acquisitiveness of their elders. Selfless dedication to one's country seemed far more appealing than a materialism which appeared to have brought privileges for the undeserving few and national disorganization and widespread unemployment to many hardworking people in Germany. Leadership for the next generation was trained in the Adolf Hitler Schools. When they were called upon to fight for their country, the Hitler Youth willingly took up the sword. H W Koch was a member of this new generation of Hitler Youth. When the fatherland was invaded, as a young boy he fought to defend his country. When the mask of Nazism was stripped away in 1945, he, like millions of others, saw what lay behind. The distance between Munich and Dachau is short; the ideological distance was vast. The shock that the world felt, and still feels about the atrocities committed in the name of national revival and self-defense was even greater for one who supported his nation in a time of disintegration and defeat. One wonders if the idealism, so apparent in the youth of the 1970s, will also be perverted to unworthy ends as the Hitler Youth was a generation ago.

This story of the origin and demise of the ideals of the Hitler Youth, a story of how youthful striving for a better world was distorted and warped by a party and government which squandered a generation and its ideals, is unusual, if not unique. H W Koch is a Lecturer in German history at the University of York and brings to this book not only his reminiscences of what it was like to be a member of the Hitler Youth; he analyzes its rise, its popularity and its complex organization with critical perception.

The background

'It has to be the aim of the volkish state to direct its educational work not for the mere purpose of the indoctrination of knowledge but to rear and train healthy bodies. Training of the intellectual faculties represents only a secondary aim. But here again the emphasis has to lie on the endeavour first of all to shape and form the character, especially to develop willpower and the ability to make decisions combined with a pronounced sense of responsibility. Scholarly and scientific training takes the last place . . . a man of small intellectual attainment, but physically healthy, of good and stable character, able to exercise his willpower and ready to make responsible decisions is a more valuable member of and asset to the national community than a highly educated weakling.'

In these sentences, as early as 1924, Adolf Hitler summarised the principles which should guide the educational policy of the national socialist state of the future and its attitude to German youth. He was sowing in fertile soil. The defeat of Germany in the First World War was not merely the defeat of the German Empire; to a young generation of frontline soldiers, and to those too young to participate in the war but old enough to observe critically what was going on around them, to that generation it was also the defeat of a stagnant society of sham-bourgeois values.

Germany's youth had begun to react against Wilhelmine society long before the First World War when it began to organise itself into youth movements which varied in shade but held in common the hope of doing away with artificial bric-à-brac some time in the unforeseeable future and breaking through towards new beginnings. It was a youth that insisted upon being led by youth, not by a moribund generation striving to re-live its second childhood. That spirit of independence

German youth on the march: the road to physical perfection led also, they believed, to strength of character

and new assertiveness caused considerable concern among bishops and socialists alike, who at first strongly resisted any attempts on the part of their denominational and party-political youth organisations to become autonomous. But they and others were unsuccessful in stemming the demand of youth to 'shape their own lives' which found its formal expression in the proclamation issued at their annual meeting at the *Hohe Meissner* mountain in October 1913.

'The Free German Youth is determined to shape its own life, to be responsible to itself and guided by the innate feeling of truth. To defend this inner liberty they close their ranks. For the sake of mutual understanding they will regularly hold Free German Youth meetings. All assemblies of the Free German Youth are free of alcohol and nicotine.'

Obviously this new, ardent generation was in no position to do away with the existing order, the old established authorities of imperial and monarchical institutions, the traditional authority of the school, the church and the home. As one avenue of escape from an environment that was felt to be oppressive they left home at week-ends and during school or university holidays, with tent, rucksack and guitar, hiking through Germany north to south, east to west, discovering for themselves the quiet beauty of the German countryside which contrasted so strongly with the belching factories of its urban centres. Their ears, alienated by the cacophony of the steel mills and forges, responded to the harmony of Beethoven's Pastoral Symphony and to Schiller's Ode to Joy. In search of something new, they turned to an age gone by, epitomised by the romantic element in most of Wagner's operas, and around the campfires they sat singing the ballads of old. Folklore experienced a renaissance.

In its basic sentiments the German

National Party Day 1935; youth club members mass at Nuremberg

The road to Cambrai 1917. On the battlefields of the First World War class barriers were broken, and the Youth Movement emerged more closely united

youth of this period was a united movement; superficial divisions such as religious denominations and class persisted, but they were no longer unbridgeable. Most of the members of the youth movements came from a middle class background but while they reacted against that background, they could never completely clear the obstacles between them and the youth movements of the organised socialists. Conversely, socialist youth movements, reacting against a party which had fossilised into an institution and a way of life determined from cradle to grave, were not yet completely at ease with their middle class contemporaries. Neither could jump over its own shadow, but at least they had begun to understand one another's problems.

When they finally did meet, ten months after the *Hohe Meissner* meeting, it was in the trenches of the First World War. From the factory floor, from classrooms and lecture halls they streamed into the army, until

during the first few weeks after the outbreak of war even the German army had to put a stop to the numbers of volunteers with which it could no longer cope. Volunteers ready to make the supreme sacrifice which they believed to be threatened by the forces of despotic Czarism and western capitalist plutocracy. Their attacks in the early months of the war were carried out with an élan that feared '*weder Tod noch Teufel*' (neither death nor devil) and their idealism found its apotheosis in November 1914, when German student volunteer companies attacked by frontal assault the British positions at Langemarck, with the words of the national anthem on their mouths, all too quickly silenced by British machine-gun fire. The attack failed, in the long term depriving the

11

German army of much-needed officer material, but it also created a myth, a myth of dedication to the Fatherland to the point of self-sacrifice, the myth of obedience to orders even if their purpose – as in the case of Langemarck – was highly questionable. The myth of Langemarck was to act as a profound influence upon Germany's youth, exerting its morbid magnetism right up to the end of the Second World War.

War created its own yardstick, the staccato of machine-gun fire and the artillery barrages forged the *aristocrazzia trencheresta*, the 'aristocracy of the trenches', and the trenches proved to be the great levelling force between classes, between officers and men, between middle class and working class. They demanded the instant readiness of individual self-sacrifice for one's comrades and they created new human relationships, a new order in which obedience in the final analysis was voluntary because he who commanded had first of all to command the respect of men who were not merely his subordinates but also his comrades.

German youth of all political convictions had reacted against the bourgeois society of Wilhelmine Germany by means of the entire spectrum of youth movements. Those who survived the war were disinclined to assist in the restoration of a society that had failed to withstand the test of war. The activists among the youth movement were to be found among the social revolutionaries of both Left and Right, among the *Spartakists* as well as in the *Freikorps*. Never united, they both fought what they considered to be the common foe, the restoration of the social *status quo*. What divided the political activists of the Left and Right was the simple fact that the latter were never prepared to destroy their own country in order to destroy capitalism, and the politically more articulate among them picked up the thread left by the German Liberal, Friedrich Naumann,

Above left: French troops raid a German trench. Until late in the war a myth persisted that German troops were eager for self-sacrifice. *Above: Spartacists* (leftist revolutionaries) are rounded up in Berlin during the 1919 riots. *Below:* Armistice conference between government troops and *Spartacists*. The revolutionary impulse was soon exhausted

Above: Barricades in Hamburg. Government troops now face their own countrymen. *Below:* Street bivouac in Berlin. The explicit rejection of the old order, earnestly desired by a large section of the population, was resisted by the establishment

endeavouring to achieve a genuine synthesis between nationalism and socialism – the antithesis between an 'unhistoric humanitarian Marxism and a rootless capitalistic system'. Some youngsters, realising that 'we had to lose the war in order to win the nation', were prepared to drive the still-born revolution of 1918 even further and remove by assassination anyone who seemed capable of restoring Germany to its pre-1914 position. Walther Rathenau was their most prominent victim, but he was sacrificed in vain. The revolutionary impulse in Germany had exhausted itself. Left and Right alike: what the public desired was a return to normality.

But youth did not want it normal. Once again they formed their own movements, movements greater in number and membership than they had ever been before the war. 'Young Socialists', 'Young Democrats', 'Young Conservatives', 'Young Protestants' are but a few of the many autonomous youth organisations that mushroomed in Germany in the wake of 1918. The cleansing of the German body politic of the abominations of industrialism, the fight against the manifold social injustices of the capitalistic system, the struggle against the *Diktat* of Versailles were points common to most of them and which played their part in the foundation of student associations such as the *Deutscher Hochschulring* or the *Deutsche Studentenschaft* or the Communist Free Proletarian Youth. Naturally, the vast number of youth organisations and their immense proliferation also reflects just how deeply Germany was divided politically. But above and beyond them were such common factors as have already been mentioned – the explicit rejection of the old, the sense of mission to create a new world for some, a new nation for others. There was a determined attempt to analyse what were thought to be the realities of the time and by direct positive action to influence them, to give them shape according to their own image, whatever that image may have been.

They also accepted the maxim coined by the German writer and poet, Walter Flex: 'Whoever swears his oath upon the Prussian flag has nothing any more that belongs to himself.' Youth organisations of the Right and Left alike sang the song written for the Communist youth by Hermann Claudius – himself later to be a National Socialist –

'When we march side by side
And sing the old songs
Resounding in the woods
We feel we shall succeed
In creating a new time.'

The youth of the front line generation which had learned at an early stage to risk their lives were prepared to do so again. One of the most articulate representatives of what could be termed 'socialism of the trenches' described their position: 'The war had exercised an all-compelling force over them, it rules them, the war would never release them, never will they be able to return home, never will they belong entirely to us. The front line experience will run forever through the current of their bloodstream, the sense of the close proximity of death, of preparedness, the horror, intoxication and steel. What now was attempted could never succeed in the first place, the attempt at integration into a peaceful, orderly and bourgeois world. This was a fraudulent transplantation which was bound to fail. The war is over, but its warriors are still on the march. And because the masses are standing here in the midst of a German world of ferment, helpless, divided into small desires and great hopes, but of significance because of the weight of their numbers and containing all the elements of nature, because of that the soldiers are marching for a revolution, for a different revolution, whether they wish it or not, driven forward by forces that escape definition, dissatisfied when they part company, highly explosive material as long as they stay together.'

Their national revolutionary attitude, hardened into conviction before the war, did not allow them even to consider the restoration of the short-lived empire gone by, nor to be convinced by its bourgeois epilogue, the Weimar Republic. The youth of the prewar movements represented during the early period of the Weimar Republic one of its vital political forces. Ironically enough, without it the young republic would hardly have survived its first six months. In the *Freikorps* those youths hardened by 'the Thunder of Steel' secured Germany's frontiers in the east, they radically suppressed the forces of separatism in the Rhineland, of particularism in Bavaria. After the occupation of the Ruhr by the French, Left and Right combined to fight the occupiers, created conspiracies, blasted separatist movements and railway bridges in the Rhineland.

One of the major shortcomings of the first German Republic was its failure to attract the youth of the German nation. It was too placid, too bourgeois and too complacent. It completely failed in its attempt to channel the restless dynamic energies of the young generation into directions which would ultimately be beneficial to the entire nation. From its very beginnings it was burdened with compromises, it cared too much for party loyalties and the vested interests of industry to elicit any spark of excitement among its youth.

Given the excess of democracy inherent in the Weimar system, Germany's ideological fragmentation was aggravated by political and economic difficulties and by the heritage of the Peace of Versailles. There were plenty of reasons which would account for an alienated generation organising itself not for but against the new republic. Already in 1919 a proclamation calling for the new organisation of the German youth movement declared: 'From a

thousand wounds our people are bleeding. We are to be deprived of all that which has made us great . . . Today every German is faced by the question: downfall or recovery – life or death? . . . Therefore we turn to Germany's youth of both sexes and all classes, to those who still attend school and those who have left it already. We appeal to them irrespective of their denominational background. We want to gather that which has been sundered apart. The existing youth movements shall continue in their work; what we want to do is to weld them into one large national youth community. But we also appeal to those hundreds of thousands who are not yet organised. We appeal to the youth of Germany as a whole.'

Little came of that appeal, nor of most other appeals which were even remotely suspected of having any connection with any of the 'established' parties. By comparison with his much more experienced rivals in the field, Hitler, from the earliest stages of his political activity, moved with much greater subtlety and conveyed much greater conviction. The simple corporal who had served in the trenches and not in the futile debates of the Reichstag, had the ability of simplification which reduced complex problems into tangible slogans. His 'national socialist' movement met the very needs of many of those who thought that a synthesis between nationalism and socialism ought to be possible. Since he neither said what he meant by 'nationalism' nor by 'socialism', he could be all things to all men. His movement, for a time at least, became the great *Sammelbecken*, the melting pot of frequently mutually exclusive concepts, personalities, and political aspirations. In this pot nationalist and socialist ideas, Herder's humanitarian concept of the Volk and

Hitler in 1923. He advocated a synthesis between nationalism and socialism which found a wide appeal

Jackboots and Swastikas: early Nazis on the march in 1923

Houston Stewart Chamberlain's racism, pan-German wish-dreams, corporate ideology and fascist leadership principles were stirred with old ideas of the *Reich* and the Prussian traditions of sobriety and obedience. That the elements in this melting pot did not fuse was another matter, but at least by comparison with the existing Reichstag parties Hitler appeared to have something new and different to offer.

His storm troopers and SS-formations attracted greater numbers of volunteers than any of the other private armies of the right-wing and left-wing parties which sprouted throughout the days of the Weimar Republic. One who at that time had not yet become a member of any of the Nazi organisations wrote 'We are now ready to create large groups and formations, which with immense strength will pursue one aim only. We are ready to subordinate ourselves to our leaders and we despise those who, typical of yesterday and of the day before care only for the superficiality of the ego, those who thought that by obeying an order coming from outside they were giving something

away. This cult of individualism of past generations, this caressing of one's own peculiarity down to the most insignificant matters, we deplore. Therefore we also despise those circles of the present bourgeoisie which are incapable of organising themselves into forceful movements, because they cannot and will not subordinate themselves, in the perpetual fear of losing a minute quantity of their own individualism.'

These are the words of a generation that had learned to sacrifice, to suffer and to kill. Too young and too involved in the turmoil around them, they did not possess the ability, or,

perhaps, the time, to cooly analyse and to judge. They were the ready-made material for the Pied Pipers of Nuremberg who promised them a new Germany, a new *Reich*, and a new society.

Long before the National Socialists had 'co-ordinated' and 'integrated' the diverse formations of the German youth movement into the Hitler Youth, Germany's young minds were permeated by attitudes and convictions which made the change of the colour of the uniform a mere formality.

The beginnings

Although from its earliest beginnings the National Socialist movement appealed for the support of Germany's youth, the actual initiative did not come from Hitler himself, or for that matter from any one of his direct subordinates. It came from a man virtually unknown, one Gustav Adolf Lenk, a piano polisher by trade, born in Munich on 15th October 1903. After the war, during the revolutionary events in Munich in 1919, he joined the 'German National Youth Movement', but gradually took exception to the middle class bias which this particular youth movement appeared to develop.

Listening to a number of speeches which Hitler delivered at Munich's *Feldherrnhalle* and at the *Hofbräuhaus*, he became one of the early converts to Nazism and joined the Nazi movement early in December 1921. Hardly in receipt of his membership card, he began addressing memoranda directly to Hitler and to Adolf Drexler, one of the founders of the NSDAP, urging the need for the foundation of a youth organisation under its auspices, and that of the SA, the storm troopers.

Hitler did not require much persuasion and in a circular issued in Munich on 22nd February, addressed to sections and sub-sections of the NSDAP and the SA, he stated: 'Because of the increase of enquiries reaching the party leadership asking whether the movement had its own youth section, we have decided to call into existence the necessary organisation for the purpose of founding a youth section.

'The statutes of the party are in no way a hindrance to this, but on the contrary carry implicit provisions for this step.

'The organisation of the youth section will be conducted by the *Sturmabteilung* which will immediately work out in detail organisational

Armed Nazis at an early rally. The Nazi Party articulated the hopes for a new society long nurtured by the post-1918 generation

statutes which upon their completion will be forwarded to the individual *Ortsgruppen* [local party districts].

'Therefore, as from now, all correspondence concerning a youth section is to be addressed to the headquarters of the SA [Administration of the NSDAP], *Sturmabteilung*, Munich 13, Corneliustrasse 12.'

This was followed by a public proclamation 'To the German Youth' published in the party's official organ, the *Voelkischer Beobachter*, on 18th March 1922, in which Hitler called for the creation of a youth movement of the NSDAP. 'The party has now called into being a "Youth Movement of the National Socialist Workers' Party" whose purpose it is to gather all our young supporters who, because of their young age cannot as yet be accepted in the ranks of the storm troopers. The movement has its own statutes, it will educate its members in the same spirit which characterises the party. We believe that the name of "movement" alone is sufficient guarantee that our youths will receive the best possible training for their difficult task in the future. Upon their shoulders rests the future of our Fatherland. The "Youth Movement of the NSDAP" will ensure that these shoulders will be strong enough some day to be able to carry this gigantic weight.

'We demand that the National Socialist youth, and all other young Germans, irrespective of class or occupation, aged between fourteen and eighteen, whose heart is affected by the suffering and hardships of the Fatherland, and who later desire to join the ranks of the fighters against the Jewish enemy, the sole originator of the present shame and suffering, enter the "Youth Movement of the NSDAP". We appeal also to youth organisations which at present are not part of any political movement, to

The first anniversary of the Third Reich is celebrated by marches and demonstrations

join this German united front against the common enemy by joining us, thus creating a mighty battering ram.

'To enable also the poorest young Germans to enter into the youth movements we shall not levy a membership fee. We expect and hope however for generous contributions from party members with greater means . . . '

This was followed a few days later by the publication of the statutes. Point I made the youth movement an integral part of party. Point II stated the existence of its own statutes, but emphasised that the spirit pervading them was the same as that of the party. It rejected any minimisation of Germany's present position, and the parliamentary point of view of 'on the one hand – on the other' and instead insisted on a relentless recognition of the truth. It was to be the movement of all those who, upon reaching their eighteenth birthday, wanted to join the storm troopers of the NSDAP.

Point III tried to articulate some of the aims of the youth movement, to reawaken and to treasure those characteristics which have their origins in the Germanic blood, namely 'love of one's country and people, enjoyment of honest open combat and of healthy physical activity, the veneration of ethical and spiritual values, and the rejection of those values originating from Jewry and Mammon'. Point III also stated that the movement ignored differences of class, occupation or social standing, since these do not correspond with true Germanic nature 'and are contradictory of the ancient concepts of a community of race and blood of all German people.'

Point IV stipulated that this 'spirit' was to be cultivated by weekly meetings, lectures, hiking trips and 'games of movement' of all kinds, while point V limited membership to 'Germans (Aryans) between the age of fourteen and eighteen years. Foreigners and Jews can not be members.' Point VI

23

emphasised that there was no membership fee while point VII explained in greater detail what had already been touched upon in general terms in point IV. There would be a meeting once a week in which lectures, discussions and talks would be held. Every second Sunday was to be spent hiking, which was compulsory. To prevent the intrusion of 'trashy literature' the youth movement would establish its own libraries which were to be continuously enlarged by the voluntary gifts of 'good books' by members of the youth movement. Point VIII required each member upon the advent of his eighteenth birthday to leave the movement. 'It is open to him then to enter the *Sturmabteilungen* of the NSDAP.' The final points, IX and X, were of a purely organisational nature.

Contrary to the initial expectation, there was no rush to join the Nazi youth movement. This reluctance can be accounted for in various ways. First of all the National Socialist

movement in 1922 was still in the main a purely local, Bavarian affair, one of the many Right-wing groupings which had been created in Bavaria after the suppression of the Bolsheviks. Though, as a result of the 'Soviet experience', anti-Semitism had become considerably more vociferous and organised than ever before, its explicit espousal in the party programme and in the statutes of its youth movement could not be sanctioned by the Catholic church which had a stronghold in Bavaria. Nor was the church anxious to encourage rivals to its own youth groups.

It took nearly another two months, until 13th May 1922, before a public meeting could be announced at which the official foundations of the 'Youth Movement of the NSDAP' were laid. The meeting, which took place in the historic *Bürgerbräukeller*, was filled to capacity. Nevertheless it was a disappointment, for among those who attended it only seventeen were youths. Speakers were Hitler himself,

Above left: Acolytes spellbound. Upon such shoulders Hitler placed the 'gigantic weight' of Germany's future. *Above:* Hiking trip in Bavaria. One of the statutes of the NSDAP emphasised the importance of physical perfection. *Below:* Future soldiers of the Third Reich accustom themselves to spartan conditions at a summer camp

the then leader of the storm troopers, the former lieutenant and *Freikorps* member Johann Ulrich Klintsch and Gustav Adolf Lenk, who was put in command of the youth movement for the Munich area, which carried the name *Jungsturm Adolf Hitler*. Its immediate superior authority was the SA and the first uniforms worn by the boys were modelled of those of the SA. Within the youth movement there were two basic divisions, one group catering for those aged between fourteen and sixteen, the other group for those between sixteen and eighteen. For this second group, uniforms were something of a problem, since they proved to be indistinguishable from the storm troopers, a point very much resented by the latter.

The *Jungsturm Adolf Hitler* made its first public appearance as a unit on the first official *Parteitag* in Munich – the party day which was to be the predecessor of those monumental fiestas of mass choreography held later in Nuremberg. There, on 28th January 1923, the youths were given their first pennants, a white flag bearing a blue anchor in the centre. The pennant was a short-lived symbol; during one of the street battles between the various political factions which were so characteristic of the Weimar Republic in general, and of Munich in particular the *Jungsturm Adolf Hitler* was involved and Munich police confiscated the pennant.

In the meantime other NS youth groups had been formed in Nuremburg, Zeitz, Dresden and Hanau. They were in the main the work of Lenk, who, although lacking any charismatic qualities of leadership, was a very able organiser. The numbers of youth groups continued to increase throughout most of 1923 and as a result Hitler promoted Lenk from his hitherto purely regional position to a 'national' one. He was to build up an administrative and organisational centre for the NS youth movement for the whole of Germany. Lenk divided the movement into provincial units

which by the summer of 1923 had risen to nine. In May 1923 the first publication of the youth movement was also distributed or reached the newsstands, entitled the *Nationale Jungsturm*. When at a very early stage it became clear that for the time being there was little future in an independent NS youth magazine, it became a regular supplement of the *Voelkischer*

Recruits parade at an administrative training centre near Salzburg

Beobachter and was re-entitled 'National Socialist Youth'.

Quite independently from Lenk's enterprise, German youths in the Sudetenland led by one Eugen Weese had founded the 'National Socialist Youth Association', while in Austria under Walter Gattermeyer and Adolf Bauer a movement called 'National Socialist Workers' Youth' was foun-ded which had groups in the Tyrol, Salzburg, Carinthia, Vienna and Lower Austria. Lenk was quick to realise the advantage of trying to bring all these groups under one central organisation. Meetings were held in Munich, Salzburg and in Eger, though it

27

Gerhard Rossbach, the founder and former leader of the *Freikorps Rossbach*, outside a Munich beer cellar

appears that neither the Sudeten Germans nor the Austro-Germans were enthusiastic about the prospect of subordinating themselves to Lenk. They sent delegations of their boys to various public functions in Munich and in Nuremburg, but that was all before the entire venture disintegrated as a result of Hitler's abortive putsch of 8th-9th November 1923 in Munich.

Just how essential Hitler was to any continued existence of the NSDAP was amply demonstrated by his absence, when he was imprisoned for nine months in the fortress of Landsberg. He alone was the lynch pin of the Nazi movement, the one man who could give it coherence and shape. After the rise of the Communist Party it was clear that there was room at the opposite end of the political spectrum for a similarly radical party to arise. That this party was the

In reflective mood, Hitler at the window of his cell in Landsburg jail

NSDAP and that it asserted its dominance over the vast proliferation of right wing parties and groupings centred solely around the personality of Hitler.

With Hitler behind the walls of Landsberg the party disintegrated and with it its youth movement. Gerhard Rossbach, the founder and former leader of the *Freikorps Rossbach*, one of Hitler's early supporters had to go into exile to Austria where he founded the *Schilljugend*, named after one of the defenders of the city of Kolberg against Napoleon's forces in 1807. Lenk founded a Youth Association Greater Germany and a German Defence Youth Association just outside northern Bavaria – a region which straddles both Thuringia and Saxony. In other regions successor organisations were camouflaged as sports or hiking associations.

29

Above: Before his imprisonment, Hitler with Alfred Rosenberg (left) and Dr Friedrich Weber of the *Oberland Freikorps. Below:* Julius Streicher, socialist revolutionary, and Adolf Hitler in Munich

The disagreements between Hitler's followers obviously affected the youth organisations as well. Gregor Strasser, against Hitler's orders, formed the National Socialist Liberty Party which participated in the Reichstag elections of May 1924, gaining twelve seats. Drexler, Alfred Rosenberg, Julius Streicher and others who represented the more social revolutionary and anti-capitalist faction within the party suspected any cooperation with the north German 'bourgeoisie' and founded their own *Grossdeutsche Volksgemeinschaft*, the Greater German National Community. Its initial leader possessed none of the organisational talents necessary at this stage; hence recourse was had to Gustav Adolf Lenk who had continued to maintain all his previous connexions.

With Hitler's release, the NSDAP was newly founded. On 4th March, 1925, Lenk published a proclamation for recreating a youth movement of the NSDAP. His restlessness and drive helped him personally very little. Quite suddenly, as yet unidentified personalities defamed his character to Hitler and he was dismissed from his post, because of alleged incapacity and embezzlement – both trumped up charges.

But Lenk's activities in the Vogtland during Hitler's absence brought their returns. One of the groups founded under his guidance was at Plauen and its leader was Kurt Gruber, born in 1904, a typical product of the German postwar generation, who saw Germany's future and restoration exclusively within the framework of the realisation of a national Socialism. Gruber was himself very active in the region and had soon established his own connection with like-minded youth groups. Equally important was the fact that he managed to raise financial support from a textile manufacturer by the name of Martin Mutschmann, who himself had become a recent member of the NSDAP and later on was to be one of its

Edmund Heines, who replaced Gustav Lenk as controller of the youth affairs of the NSDAP

*Gauleiter*s. With that support Gruber organised the NS youth movement throughout Saxony. Outside Munich this was the largest NS youth group, while for the time being attempts in Berlin and in Prussia remained unsuccessful.

Gruber's success was mainly due to the degree of independence which he preserved for himself. He warded off any interference from the party headquarters in Munich, and in 1925 after the NSDAP had been refounded, he called a meeting at Plauen of all Saxon leaders of the youth movement. At this meeting the Greater German Youth Association, whose largest component was that of Gruber, formally became part of the NSDAP and all connections which existed with other similarly orientated youth organisations were severed, because Hitler rejected any movement which did not subject itself unconditionally to his personal will.

In place of Lenk, Edmund Heines, a former lieutenant and member of the Freikorps Rossbach, was appointed to deal with the youth affairs of the NSDAP. Heines had been one of the leaders of the *Schilljugend* which, via

31

other nationalist youth groups as well as the boy scouts, had expanded into Bavaria. This appointment immediately produced a conflict which remained unresolved throughout the early history of the Nazi Party. The *Schilljugend* had a reputation as an élitist, predominantly middle-class body. Gruber, whose adherents were mainly working class youths from the industrial districts of Saxony and Thuringia, immediately argued that an absorption of the Greater German Youth Association into the *Schilljugend* would narrow down its base of recruitment, for no working class youth was likely to join the snobbish *Schilljugend*. At best, he would agree to join the latter on condition that his youth groups would retain their original name. The *Schilljugend* refused, emphasizing its élitist character. This pushed Hitler's support in Gruber's direction, who confirmed him on 2nd October, 1925 as the 'Leader of the National Socialist Youth Movement for Saxony'. When in 1926 Rossbach was amnestied and could return to Germany he was no longer prepared to subordinate himself to Hitler and went his own way. However, it was precisely the élitist concept underlying the *Schilljugend* that ultimately caused its disintegration.

Ideologically, Gruber was a simpleton. He took Hitler's programme as he read it, unaware of its inherent ambiguities and interpreting the more uncompromising anti-semitic statements as the veneer of the times, the radical implications of which would soon wear off once its propagandist effect had been achieved. Hitler's support of his position against the *Schilljugend* seemed to confirm his assessment of Hitler as a social revolutionary and as long as he retained that conviction he was ready to obey Hitler's every command. From Hitler's point of view, a man like Gruber could much more easily be handled than the representatives of the former frontline officers, men like Captain Ernst Röhm, Stennes or Rossbach.

On the first Party-rally of the resurrected party, held on 3rd and 4th July 1926 at Weimar at the suggestion of Julius Streicher, the *Gauleiter* of Franconia, the Greater German Youth Association was renamed the *Hitler-Jugend*, League of the German Workers' Youth. The *Hitler-Jugend*, the HJ, was born. Simultaneously the Hitler Youth was declared by Hitler to be the only official youth organisation of the NSDAP, and Gruber was appointed its first *Reichsführer* as well as adviser for youth questions in the Party HQ.

In practice this meant the integration into the party apparatus of the previously independent NS youth movement. Gruber's own position was now that of a party official and no longer that of an independent youth leader who could take such initiatives as he desired to take. On the other hand the 'National Socialist Workers' Youth' which had existed in Austria since 1923 accepted integration into the Hitler Youth as did many other similar groups inside Germany. Consequently Gruber's field of activity was no longer restricted to Saxony but included the whole of Germany and Austria. Hence his immediate task was to facilitate the process of integration as smoothly as possible – in which, on the whole, he succeeded.

Out of isolated units strewn across the whole of Germany emerged one organisation. But more difficult, as the following years were to show, was the complete integration of the Hitler Youth into the party apparatus. When in November 1926 the former *Freikorps*-leader Captain Franz Felix Pfeffer von Salomon was appointed by Hitler as commander of the SA (OSAF) he immediately demanded that the Hitler Youth be subject to SA command, to which, in spite of some grumbling by Gruber, Hitler readily agreed. A month later Gruber called the first meeting of the leaders of the Hitler Youth at Weimar which was also attended by Pfeffer. Exercising considerable tact and an approach

Above: Julius Streicher speaking at Weimar on the first Party Day of the resurrected party, 4th July 1926. *Below:* Captain Franz Felix Pfeffer von Salomon (on Hitler's left) at a rally in Nuremberg in 1927. As commander of the SA, he demanded that the Hitler Youth be subject to SA command

Hitler reviews an SA unit at Weimar on the 1926 Party Day

of paternal friendship Pfeffer quickly managed to calm all of Gruber's suspicions and turn him into a ready collaborator. The practical result of this meeting was the issue of 'Guidelines concerning the relationship between the NSDAP and the HJ' which were signed by Pfeffer on behalf of the NSDAP and by Gruber on behalf of the Hitler Youth.

In essence these reaffirmed the main provisions of statutes of 1922, which of course, had lapsed in the meantime. But there were also important additions such as, for instance, that any 'Hitler Youth' member above the age of eighteen had to be a party member and that the loss of party membership automatically included the loss of Hitler Youth membership as well. This meant that all higher functionaries of the Hitler Youth had to be party members. The organisation of the Hitler Youth was fitted into the

structure of that already existing for the NSDAP, and mainly that of the SA, i.e. *Gau* (province or part of a province) *Bezirk* (region) and *Ortsgruppe* (district). All appointments to the higher ranks of the Hitler Youth required the agreement of the NSDAP as did any one of its public appearances. The Hitler Youth had to follow any command issued by a party leader and quarterly meetings of its leadership were to be held under NSDAP guidance. For the first time a membership fee of four pfennigs per month was to be levied. Uniforms were to be standardised with special emphasis on the avoidance of any confusion with the uniform of the storm troopers.

Between 1926 and 1933 the major preoccupation of the Hitler Youth appears to have been to assert its own position inside the NSDAP, which some members considered simply that of an appendix of the SA, others as boy scouts of a National Socialist vintage, while within the Hitler

October 1927. Within the committee's competence lay also National Socialist student associations and since the committee's responsibilities continued to grow, in 1928 it was transformed into the 'Youth Office' of the NSDAP headed by Walter Buch, a former major and the chairman of the party's investigation and arbitration committee. This immediately produced conflicts over the respective responsibilities concerning the Hitler Youth between the Youth Office and the SA leadership, conflicts which finally were resolved in favour of the Hitler Youth and the Youth Office. Actually Pfeffer himself had unwittingly assisted his own defeat when, late in 1927, he had given way to Gruber's persistent complaints about the lack of trained leadership in the upper echelons of the Hitler Youth, by allowing the organisation to retain such members in its ranks who, although they had attained the age of eighteen, would be further required.

Gruber now believed that the way was clear, the state of dependency on the SA had been eliminated, and the Hitler Youth could go on developing its own character and traditions. The absence of the latter was often felt among the rank and file who did not even have their own 'youth movement' songs and therefore had to sing those of its 'bourgeois nationalist' rivals or not sing at all. Early in 1928, still receiving more financial support from private sources than from the party itself. Gruber installed the 'Reichs Administrative Office of the Hitler Youth' in Plauen. All the work done there was voluntary and unpaid, but in spite of that Gruber could extend the activities of his office by establishing a separate section for the 'frontier regions'. This section took up the old connections first established by Lenk with the Sudeten German groups in Czechoslovakia and also some of the German minority groups in Poland. To introduce some kind of 'inner solidarity' within the

Youth itself the tendency towards being commanded by members of an older generation gave cause for complaint, since it offended the fundamental maxim of all German youth movements at the time – that youth must be led by youth. This also made the Hitler Youth vulnerable to the criticism of other youth movements and caused the first 'secession' within it when in May 1927 in Northern Germany a radical wing separated, dropping the name HJ and changing it to 'League of German Workers' Youth'.

Although the 'guidelines' of 1926 implied simultaneous membership of the Hitler Youth and the NSDAP, the old practice still continued whereby each member, upon reaching the age of eighteen, had to leave the Hitler Youth and could become a member of the SA. This seriously restricted the training of a body of indigenous Hitler Youth leaders for the upper ranks. This was one of the first problems discussed by the 'Youth Committee of the NSDAP' founded in

Amateur trumpeters at a *Jungvolk*
meeting. Hitler set up the *Jungvolk*
as a junior extension to the Hitler
Youth

Hitler Youth, special days of the year
were allocated when at the same time
throughout Germany all Hitler Youth
units would assemble to listen to a
special order of the day or policy
proclamation.

On 19th December 1928 Gruber
called a meeting for the entire Hitler
Youth leadership at Plauen, on which
occasion three major problems were
discussed: the setting up of junior
groups of the Hitler Youth which
would comprise those aged between
ten and fourteen, later to become the
Jungvolk; the foundation of girl formations within the Hitler Youth,
later known as the BDM, the League
of German Girls; and lastly the
setting out of principles which clearly
defined the separateness of the Hitler
Youth from other nationalist youth
groups. Gruber insisted that the

Hitler Youth should be compared as
little with any other existing youth
group as the NSDAP with any other
party. It was neither a political para-
military association, nor an association of 'anti-semitic boy scouts', nor
for that matter part of any of the
other bodies of the existing fossilised
youth movement. It was a 'new youth
movement of young social revolutionary minded Germans' who felt
themselves deeply at one with the
fate of their nation.

Its major aim was the training of
the individual personality to face and
master the existing circumstances.
This did not simply mean to experience one's country, but to fight for it,
putting at stake one's own life to
liberate it from 'the shackles of
capitalists and the enemies of the
German race'. It therefore followed
that the new socialist national community of Hitler's conception could
only be created over the dead body of
Marxism. Gruber denounced the sec-
tarianism of other youth movements

and implied that they would be superseded by an all-embracing Hitler Youth.

Gruber's renewed emphasis on the separateness of the Hitler Youth was not just the expression of a personal whim, but was based on experience. Outside the Hitler Youth the National Socialist Student Movement had been founded which by the end of 1928 was led by Baldur von Schirach who used this as his base of power from which he hoped to bring about the fusion of all nationalist youth groups. Naturally enough Gruber considered this not only as a challenge to his own position but also to his own conception of the Hitler Youth.

Schirach was born in 1907, the son of a former Prussian captain and later administrator of the Court Theatre at Weimar. His mother was American by birth, as was his grandmother on his father's side. All the children of the Schirach family were sent to highly exclusive schools – an education which was interrupted by Germany's defeat in 1918. One of Baldur von Schirach's brothers killed himself because he did not wish to survive Germany's humiliation. The other children had to change over to local grammar schools. In 1928, while still a grammar school pupil, he heard Hitler speak for the first time, and when hardly eighteen years of age he became a member of Hitler's party. When, two years later, he had completed his matriculation he entered Munich University to read German and History of Art. Hitler himself, always flattered whenever what he took to be the upper levels of German society paid their respects to him, welcomed Schirach with open arms.

Members of the League of German Girls await a visit from their *Reichsjugendführer,* **Baldur von Schirach**

Baldur von Schirach. He used the National Socialist Student Movement as a base from which he hoped to unite all nationalist youth groups

Already in 1925 he had paid his first social call to the family, and the father soon followed the son into the party.

At Munich young Schirach became a stormtrooper though he experienced frequent ridicule because of his exclusive schoolboy image, one that he was to retain until the last days of the Third Reich. He also joined the National Socialist Student Association then led by a sincere national socialist revolutionary, Wilhelm Tempel. Schirach, who had never had to earn his own income, was totally out of touch with the world of the working class and hence came increasingly to be identified as the spokesman of the upper middle class element within the Student Association. Thanks to Hitler's active support, he became the leader of the NS Student Association in Munich and on 20th July 1928 replaced Wilhelm Tempel as *Reichsführer* and adviser for student affairs in the party headquarters. He was now intent upon obtaining the leadership of the entire Hitler Youth.

Without the knowledge of either Hitler or Gruber he sent out circulars to other youth groups. Although meant to be confidential, news of Schirach's attempts and his endeavour soon became public, much to the relish of the publications of other nationalist youth groups. Gruber did his utmost to prevent this development, travelling from one part of Germany to the other; and visiting individually every one of the leading Hitler Youth subordinates, he used all the powers of persuasion he could muster to convince them of his own viewpoint and the danger inherent in that of Schirach. In order to create a favourable impression on Hitler he made sure that on the *Reichsparteitag* 1929 in Nuremberg 2,000 Hitler youths in their brown shirts marched past 'their Führer'. Almost half of them had come from Austria, followed by Saxony, Berlin-Brandenburg and lower Saxony. The Berlin contingent created a precedent by its Adolf-Hitler March; it marched by foot the entire distance from Berlin – some 400 miles.

But Schirach had not remained inactive either. At Nuremberg he held, together with Alfred Rosenberg, a special meeting with the leaders of other nationalist groups. Gruber refused to attend and sent his deputy instead. At this meeting Shirach failed to get the support of his nationalist rivals which would automatically have meant their subordination to the Hitler Youth. With the support of the leader of stormtroopers, Pfeffer von Salomon, Hitler was won over too, and a statement issued to the effect that in future Schirach and Rosenberg were instructed that only the Hitler Youth would represent the National Socialist youth movement.

Gruber's position seemed secure once again, but on the other hand relations with most of the other nationalist youth groups had further deteriorated: and Schirach's Student Association possessed a much greater flexibility which allowed it to extend considerably its area of operations.

Above: Baldur von Schirach presents a prize at a youth club meeting. *Below:* Nazi Party Day 1929. Crowds in the market square at Nuremberg reaffirm their allegiance to the Party

The new spirit 1929-1936

In autumn 1929 Gruber applied for membership for the Hitler Youth of the 'Reichskommitee of German Youth Associations'. The application was rejected mainly on the grounds that on the basis of its statutes the Hitler Youth refused to cooperate with other youth associations and negated the existing state.

This was one mark of the growing tension of the political atmosphere ever since the onset of the depression, and Gruber, in order that the non-political German public should be made aware of the value of the Hitler Youth, moved into the public view himself. In November 1929 he successfully arranged a Hitler Youth Exhibition in Munich. In March 1930 the Hitler Youth held a mass meeting in Berlin under the heading 'From Resistance to Attack' on which occasion the most prominent speaker was the Gauleiter of Berlin, Joseph Goebbels himself.

Organisationally, the Hitler Youth was now divided into thirty-five *Gaue* (Provinces) comprising approximately 18,000 German youths and nearly 3,000 Austrians. The organisational structure was occasionally tampered with in order to make more boys available to assist in the Reichstag election campaigns.

The growing radicalization of the politics of the Weimar Republic was of course most blatant at the two extremes of the political spectrum. At first the government did its best to curb the growing extremism. In various regions the pupils of state grammar and vocational schools were forbidden to become members and contravention meant expulsion. This was followed by an ordinance for Prussia as a whole which proscribed all National Socialist as well as Communist Youth Associations. Other regional governments in Germany followed suit. During that period

Propaganda Minister, Dr Goebbels (right), and Baldur von Schirach at a Hitler Youth rally in Berlin

Young Hitler youth members – an admiring audience for the Reich's weapons of destruction

internal disputes within the NSDAP had only minor effects on the Hitler Youth which by that time was already well integrated into the NSDAP.

More serious than actual proscription was the banning of the publications of the Hitler Youth, since this, together with other proscriptions of Nazi party publications threatened an enforced idleness on the party-owned printing presses. During its early period a supplement to the *Voelkischer Beobachter* was issued, and subsequently various other publications appeared until in 1929 *Die Junge Front*, 'The Young Front', was published – a journal for Hitler Youth Leaders. Austria published its own journals. Berlin's Hitler Youth was the first to publish a fortnightly newspaper entitled, *Der Junge Sturmstrupp*, 'The Young Stormtroop'. Given the infancy of all these journals and newspapers,

their frequent proscription by regional governments as well as by the Berlin government involved serious financial losses.

Baldur von Schirach used the difficulties of the Hitler Youth as illustrations of Gruber's shortcomings as a tactician, whose stubbornness prevented the closing of the ranks of all nationalist youth movements. This of course ignored the fact that during Bruening's tenure as Chancellor between 1930 and 1932 the whole Nazi party was subjected to official pressure in order to curb its radicalism.

But during 1931 Gruber's position was declining. Röhm had returned from Bolivia where he had been employed as military instructor. Pfeffer von Salomon's aristocratic independence as SA leader began to needle Hitler, and as the tension between the two men mounted Pfeffer thought it advisable to resign his post which Hitler immediately assumed. The elections of September 1930 brought the NSDAP 6,500,000 votes and 107 seats in the

Reichstag. Röhm was appointed as Chief of Staff of the SA early in 1931, and the position of supreme leader of the SA Hitler retained for himself.

With Röhm's appointment came also a new definition of the relationship between SA and the Hitler Youth. Dated 27th April 1931, the Hitler Youth as an organisation in its own right was again put under the direct command of the Supreme SA leadership and the *Reichsführer* HJ was made a subordinate of the Chief of Staff of the SA.

All Hitler Youth groups were subordinated to the regional SA commander but not to other SA branches or offices. The function of SA guidance of the Hitler Youth was restricted to guidance of the HJ in public marches or any other public demonstration, supervision of its general outside appearance, and the right to oppose a Hitler Youth appointment of the upper ranks. Each regional SA headquarters was to have its own Hitler Youth adviser, while the *Reichsführer* HJ acted in this capacity in the central headquarters of the SA in Munich. The Hitler Youth headquarters was to be transferred from Plauen to the NSDAP headquarters in Munich.

This directive eliminated the previous practice of parallel orders being issued by an SA and an HJ leader – for the middle and lower ranks they now came directly from a Hitler Youth leader, which brought about a greater liberty of movement and development for the lower echelons of the HJ. Nevertheless, the transfer of the HQ of the Hitler Youth from Plauen to Munich put an end to independence as Gruber had so far managed to preserve for himself. With the resignation of Preffer and the appointment of Röhm, Gruber's situation deteriorated, if for no other reason than that the two men could not get on with one another. Gruber's resignation followed in October 1931, thus offering ample scope to the rumour-mongers who spread false reasons for his departure such as the embezzlement of Hitler Youth funds, but there was no substance to

Ernst Röhm, appointed Chief of Staff of the SA early in 1931

them. Of greater importance was the fact that Baldur von Schirach managed to get on well with Röhm, and could point (not without foundation) to the rapid growth of his National Socialist Student Association, compared with which the growth of the Hitler Youth had been slow. Unlike Lenk, Gruber was not sent into the wilderness. A minor post was found for him as an economic adviser, and some tribute – then as well as later – was paid to his work.

The day following Gruber's 'resignation' Hitler issued a further directive in which he established the Office of the *Reichsjugendführer* within the framework of the Supreme SA leadership. The *Reichsjugendführer* was directly responsible to the Chief of Staff of the SA and the man appointed was Baldur von Schirach. Within the field of competence of the *Reichsjugendführer* came the Hitler Youth, The National Socialist Student Association and the National Socialist Pupil's League. A separate *Reichsführer* for the Hitler Youth was named, but this was a purely transitory appointment. Schirach at long last achieved his immediate objective.

The young girls of Germany also had their own organization when the *Bund Deutscher Madchen* was founded

The Hitler Youth as an organisation now acquired the National Socialist Pupil's League, which had been founded in Hamburg in 1929. Essentially oriented to the middle class, it mainly comprised pupils of secondary schools, who with a considerable degree of snobbery looked down on their proletarian brethren from the Hitler Youth. Politically they had acted with greater independence from party HQ than the Hitler Youth itself and were notorious for their anti-semitism; Jewish teachers and heads of schools found them increasingly not merely a nuisance but a definite danger. They did not refrain from physically as well as verbally attacking teachers because of their race or political convictions, thus supplying ample ammunition to those who proposed drastic steps against the menace of Hitler and his movement. As it happened the 'drastic steps' were never taken; banning and proscription only acted as pin-pricks which ultimately caused even greater and more violent reactions.

What is noticeable in Hitler's direc-

tive of 30th October 1931 is the total absence of any reference to the NS girls association – the BDM. Called into existence first in 1927 in Plauen, the girls' association vegetated in relative obscurity until July 1930 when it was formally named *Bund Deutscher Mädchen* (BDM), but it was to be another two years before directives were issued making it an integral part of the Hitler Youth and the sole girls' organisation of the NSDAP. Its growth was fairly rapid. At a Hitler Youth meeting held in October 1931, of the 70,000 attending 15,000 were girls.

Another youth organisation which joined the Hitler Youth, the *Deutsches Jungvolk*, was not founded inside Germany at all but had its roots in Austria and the Sudetenland of Czechoslovakia, but it still carried on many of the traditions of the pre-war German youth movement. Its slogans contained much that infers the influence of social revolutionary tendencies; politically it was not affiliated to any political party but it nevertheless had a right-wing bias. In Vienna it became

Camp fires and ballad singing – Schirach believed that the national pride of the under-14s was to be developed in this way

44

notorious for the part it played in its demonstrations against the film *All Quiet on the Western Front*. From 1930 onwards, those *Jungvolk* groups inside Germany began to join the Hitler Youth, not as an integral part but as a separate body within the HJ. Schirach could point here to an organisation which, within the Hitler Youth, was continuing the traditions of the German Youth movement. In practice he considered it an ideal unit which would cater for the age group up to fourteen, in which the romanticism of the camp fires and ballad singing would find good response. Out of the total youth organisations absorbed into the Hitler Youth the *Jungvolk* was the only one which was allowed to retain its colours: a black cloth centred by one victory rune (the SS was later to have two). But as the flow of units of the *Jungvolk* continued to grow, membership was forbidden in

Berlin SA members defy the ban on uniforms

A Hitler Youth contingent on the march in Berlin

many areas of Germany until, between 13th April and 16th June 1932, together with all other uniformed bodies of the NSDAP, it was completely forbidden throughout Germany.

The price of the Hitler Youth's active political involvement, particularly between 1931 and 1933, was the loss of twenty-six lives. 'We march for Hitler through the night and suffering . . . our flag means more to us than death'; the words of the 'Hitler Youth Anthem' written by Baldur von Schirach became bitter reality for some as the political struggle moved away from an impotant Reichstag into the streets, where members of the Red Front and the Brown Shirts faced one another in bitter enmity.

The most prominent victim – prominent because of the propaganda Goebbels made of the case and the film based on his life made after 1933 – was

The funeral of Herbert Norkus, Hitler Youth member murdered by Communists in Berlin in 1932

Herbert Norkus. The son of a Berlin taxi driver who, affected seriously by the depression, had joined the storm-troopers himself, he was twelve years old when as a Hitler Youth member, he was sent out on the morning of Sunday 26th January 1932 to post bills advertising an assembly. At this assembly, to be held four days later, prominent Hitler Youth leaders were to speak on such topics as 'Swastika or Soviet Star?' and 'What we want'. Norkus lived in the district of Wedding in Berlin, the 'red' Wedding as it was generally known and on that cold January morning at five o'clock he was with a Hitler Youth troop pasting posters on the walls of the streets of Berlin-Wedding. A motor cyclist passed them, returned, passed again and then disappeared into the dark. Then suddenly the bill posters were confronted by a troop of Communists and

the boys scattered in all directions. Norkus was caught and stabbed twice; he had enough strength to make another run for a house, but its owner locked the door in his face. He was stabbed again but tried to pull himself up, leaving a bloody trail as his left hand groped for support along the wall of a house. His assassins dragged him along the corridor of 4 Zwinglistrasse and left him there to die. At the Moabit Hospital the autopsy revealed five stabs in the back, two in the chest, his face had been mutilated beyond recognition and the upperlip was missing.

Such were the politics of the pluralist consensus during the last phase of the Weimer Republic. In Berlin alone six Hitler Youths were killed, three of whom came from the 'red' Wedding district. No doubt the militant opposition to the Nazis fared little better in those days, but in view of sacrifices of blood made by ideologically misguided but nevertheless idealistic young people, it would be a grave injustice to all victims of that period to classify them on the one hand as a humanitarian socialist heroes, and on the other as fascist beasts. Equally tragic is the fact that examples like that of Herbert Norkus, were further grist to Goebbel's propaganda mills, which directed the orientation and outlook of age groups yet to be born.

To obtain correct figures for the strength of the Hitler Youth at any time before 1936 and expecially for the years between 1930 and 1933 is still impossible, since few figures exist of the membership of the youth organisations such as the *Jungvolk* which up to 1933 still led a somewhat independent existence within the framework of the Hitler Youth. To use, for instance, membership fees as an indicator of membership would produce a false picture because as a result of the vast unemployment which heavily affected school-leavers (then in the age groups between fourteen and eighteen) Hitler Youths without employment paid no fees. In 1931 there were approximately 20,000 paying members but an unknown number of 'non-fee-paying' members. Berlin, which under Arthur Axmann had a highly organised Hitler Youth organisation, shows less than 1,000 fee-paying members for 1932.

Equally difficult to determine during that period are the social origins of Hitler Youth members. 1930 figures show the recruitment of 2,800 fee-paying members for the Hitler Youth, which at that time meant only the original HJ and not the BDM, the National Socialist Pupils' League, the *Jungvolk* and other similar organisations. Of these approximately 1,000 are stated to have been of working class background, over 500 pupils of various institutes of secondary education, 400 recruits from other youth movements (which allows of course no conclusion as to their social background) and 900 'others'. For 1932 more detailed but no verifiable figures are supplied – sixty-nine per cent workers, ten per cent engaged in trade and commerce (which would mean that they were

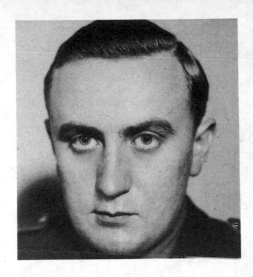

Arthur Axmann, the highly competent leader of the Berlin division of the Hitler Youth

apprentices in the commercial professions), twelve per cent school pupils. The remainder had not been determined, but it is clear that many of them were unemployed.

The depression which had helped to bring about such a landslide vote for Hitler caused also a renewed emphasis within the Hitler Youth upon the 'socialist' component and style of its agitation, particularly in urban working class areas. Berlin-Wedding was but one example. Kiel, the city and harbour from which the revolution of 1918 began, was another. There the Hitler Youth was largely ignored by the NSDAP and had to stand on its own feet. Members organised their own discussions and public speeches and protected their own meetings. The local party organisation thought of them only when they required bill posters. As in other German cities, so in Kiel, the Hitler Youth organised the systematic disruption of the film *All Quiet on the Western Front* which was thought to degrade the 'heroic image' of the German soldier. Street battles with the organised Communist Youth Associations, or for that matter with the Communist Party's own

NORTH SEA

DENMARK

BALTIC SEA

LITHUANIA

Danzig

Königsberg

EASTLAND

Hamburg

NORTH

Bremen

EAST

BERLIN

POLAND

NETHERLANDS

BELGIUM

NORTH-WEST

Cologne

CENTRE

Leipzig

Breslau

SILESIA

LUX.

WEST

Frankfurt

SAAR

Nuremberg

CZECHOSLOVAKIA

FRANCE

Stuttgart

SOUTH-WEST

SOUTH

MUNICH

Vienna

SWITZERLAND

AUSTRIA

ITALY

Boundary of Germany, 1931

Hitler Youth (HJ) Group boundary

| 0 | Miles | 200 |
| 0 | Kilometres | 300 |

Structural organisation of the Hitler Youth in 1931

para-military formation, *'Rotfront'*, were a regular occurence. For both sides fists, sticks and truncheons were no longer enough, and fire arms were often used.

When the NSDAP's para-military formations were forbidden, which in practice meant that they could not wear their uniforms, the Nazi apprentices of the butchery trade in Kiel simply wore their working garb and were particularly feared for their ferocity. Even the adult members of *'Rotfront'* were anxious not to get involved with them. In Kiel as elsewhere the Communists were their main target. In a leaflet from the summer of 1932 they made the following appeal: 'Fellow Youths. We shall overthrow the old system. We are not begging for your votes in the Reichstag election, what we want is you. On the day of the National Socialist seizure of power begins the German Revolution. Then the young socialist forces from all camps must be united to face the forces of reaction. Our banners do not carry the slogans of "Moscow", nor "Internationalism" nor "Pacifism". The only name they carry is that of "Germany" and nothing but "Germany"!

'With your banner flying, come to us the German Workers' Youth [HJ], fight with us against the old system, against the old order, against the old generation. We are the last fighters for liberty, fight with us for Socialism, for freedom and for bread!

'Join the German Workers' Youth, Kiel!'

Propaganda marches were organised through the towns and villages of Schleswig-Holstein, a region which had already been radicalized as a result of vast mortgage foreclosures because farmers were no longer able to pay their taxes. The farmers organised themselves into self-defence units which first prevented the bailiffs from driving away stock or taking possession of farms, and ultimately led to the blowing up of local tax offices.

In the countryside the Hitler Youth was tolerated, if not welcomed, and since the Communists also supported the farmers' actions a tacit truce existed there between 'red' and 'brown'. But in the towns the situation was different. The street violence caused any member of the Hitler Youth to become suspect at school, or, if he was employed, at his place of work. Parents worried about the physical wellbeing of their own children and tried to oppose their political activities, but usually in vain. Teachers were asked by local authorities to compile lists of 'Nazis' in their classes.

The Roman Catholic Church opposed the Hitler Youth in pastoral letters and various other directives, as well as by the strict control of its own youth organisations. The obscene racial anti-Semitism of Julius Streicher combined with the anti-Christian philosophy of Alfred Rosenberg, expounded in his book *The Myth of the Twentieth Century*, provided welcome vulnerable points at which one could attack the Nazi party and any one of its affiliated organisations.

On the other hand, however, the Nationalist component of the Nazis was impossible to tackle. In their desire to liberate themselves from 'the shackles' of Versailles, to recreate a new Germany, in their recognition of the impotence of the Weimar system denominational youth organisations and the Hitler Youth were at one. One of their principle aims was to create *'Grossdeutschland'*, a Germany which would include German Austria whose parliament had voted on three occasions in favour of the motion that German-Austria is a constituent part of the German Republic. Many Catholics as well as Protestants considered that the western form of democracy, the politics of a pluralist consensus, were unsuited and alien to the German political tradition, and favoured the establishment of some form of corporate state. It is no accident that the most outstanding German theoreticians of the corporate state were also devout Roman Catholics.

As a defence against the attacks

from the churches the NSDAP and its youth movement pointed to the Italian example, where Mussolini had been able to obtain the support of the Vatican, and thus establish a workable church-state relationship, and argued that all they wanted was what the church and state had established in Italy. No doubt, many members wanted just that, but this again points to the heterogenity of the forces contained within the NDSAP whose common denominator ultimately was not Germany, but one man – Adolf Hitler.

Finally, also, the elements which the denominational youth organisations had in common with the Hitler Youth led to the former adapting Hitler Youth practices, in order to forestall defections. Para-military field exercises were introduced as well as rifle shooting, though within the Catholic Youth movement one circular issued stated that the gospel and rifle practice were hardly compatible with one another. But this was a voice in the wilderness. One of the most widely sung and most notorious Hitler Youth songs was composed by a youth who at the time of its composition was still a member of the Catholic Youth. The song – '*Es zittern die morschen Knochen*' ended with the well-known refrain usually quoted as – '*denn heute gehört uns Deutschland und morgen die ganze Welt*', – 'because today Germany belongs to us and tomorrow the whole world'. In fact in youthful exuberance and aggressiveness the refrain was often sung as quoted, but its actual words were – '*denn heute da hört uns Deutschland und morgen die ganze Welt*' – 'because today Germany listens to us'[to our warning of the danger of the 'red menace'] 'and tomorrow the whole world'.

The Protestant Youth movements

Ultimately all the various denominational youth movements in Germany were to find that they had one thing in common – the belief that Hitler could lead Germany to a new era of greatness

were easier to infiltrate by the Hitler Youth than were those of the Catholics. For one thing they were much more fragmented in organisation as well as in their ideological and party political orientations, and their members ranged from ultra-German national Conservatives to Liberals. Some of them carried as their banner not the colours of the republic but those of the empire, black white and red. It is also important to make a distinction here between the leadership of the Protestant Youth movements and its membership. While the former largely retained an attitude either of reserve or even of outspoken hostility to the NSDAP, the membership was much more receptive to Hitler Youth propaganda. They, as one of their leaders put it, 'were pervaded by something irrational, infectous, which brings the blood into motion and induces the feeling that something really great was about to happen, a forceful current of which one wants to be part . . .' However, in both cases, the Hitler Youth was not able to reap the full fruits of the seeds of political radicalization until after January 1933.

1932 had brought great membership gains. A large Hitler Youth meeting was planned in Braunschweig, but forbidden by Wilhelm Groener, once Ludendorff's successor, then Minister of the Interior as well as Reichswehrminister. Instead, a closed meeting of Hitler Youth leaders took place in which colours for individual Hitler Youth units were handed over with the words 'We dedicate our flags in the sign of resurrection. May God bless our banners, for the final victory we fight ourselves.'

While Bruening was still in office as Chancellor, though governing by presidential decree and, in view of the impotent and deadlocked Reichstag, without parliamentary consent, the Republic was still strong enough to ward off the extremes of both Left and Right from taking control of the state. When Bruening was ousted and replaced by von Papen one of the first

Franz von Papen. One of his first actions as Chancellor was to revoke the ban on uniformed appearances of the military groups within the SA

actions of his chancellorship was to revoke the decrees forbidding the uniformed appearance of the paramilitary formations of the NSDAP. He hoped by means of 'an opening to the right' to obtain the support of the NSDAP in the Reichstag and with it a stable parliamentary majority. Hitler took the concessions and interpreted them correctly for what they were: a sign of weakness.

Since the late 1920s the Reichswehr had given active support to paramilitary training of Right-wing youth organisations, a support also extended to the Hitler Youth but withdrawn under Groener who endeavoured to fuse the para-military associations of all parties into one body directly under the control of the Reichswehr and Ministry of the Interior. Hitler was not prepared to put his stormtroopers and the Hitler Youth under any such control but preferred proscription. With the revocation of the prohibition in June 1932 cooperation between Hitler Youth and Reichswehr was resumed, but for the NSDAP this was of less importance than being able once again to march in uniformed for-

mations through the cities and the countryside of Germany. The Papen government now also assisted the Hitler Youth to enter the 'Reichs Committee of German Youth Associations' which had previously turned down the HJ's application for membership. But Schirach was not content with simple membership, he intended to turn the Reichs Committee into an instrument of the Hitler Youth. In his application which listed for membership the Hitler Youth, the National Socialist Student Federation, the National Socialist Pupils' League, and the League of German Girls, he stated a total membership of 120,000, of which 70,000 were Hitler Youth members. It seems likely that the figures were exaggerated.

The application was accepted. To show off the strength of the Hitler Youth, Schirach called a *Reichsjugendtag der NSDAP* at Potsdam, a rally of all German Hitler Youths. For Schirach and the Hitler Youth it proved a tremendous success, in spite of the fact that the NSDAP's coffers provided only very limited funds since these were needed to fight the new Reichstag election in November. The expected number of participants had been calculated at around 20,000, but when they arrived they were nearly 100,000 boys and girls. Only fifty large tents were available, and nearby empty factories provided sleeping space. Hitler Youth groups from all over Germany hired buses and lorries, paying back the rentals in instalments. The journey to Potsdam was in itself an impressive propaganda campaign. As soon as they entered a hamlet, village or town, the banners were unfurled on the lorries, bugle signals resounded through the streets followed by rousing marching songs. None but those ideologically opposed to the movement could fail to respect the enthusiasm and the élan of the brownshirted youths.

Boys demonstrate their agility and fitness at the Potsdam rally, attended by all Hitler Youth groups in Germany

The first camp evening took place on 1st October. Reveille was at five o'clock next morning. Later Baldur von Schirach laid a wreath at the steps of the Garrison Church of Potsdam, the shrine of Prussia, which held the coffins of two of its greatest kings, Frederick William I and Frederick the Great. Then, while 50,000 girls had assembled at Potsdam's great parade ground, the march past of the boys began at eleven o'clock, lasting until six o'clock in the evening. Unexpectedly it was Hitler himself who stood on the review stand. Even observers from other German youth organisations were impressed. 'This was more than just a party youth movement which we saw marching in Potsdam... The NSDAP has succeeded in attracting to a large measure the best blood of the young generation and to infuse it with the sacred flame of faith and enthusiasm.' Hitler's speech was the high point of the meeting and in it he stressed that Germans had to learn again to stand above their social status, their profession and their religious denomination, and to attach primary importance to their role within the national community. Germany fell, ran the thesis, because Germans had forgotten this and it was up to Germany's youth to feel again as brothers and sisters of one nation. If the Hitler Youth remained true to the maxims postulated by Hitler at Potsdam, the observer concluded 'then the Germany of tomorrow will be socialist'. Schirach stated that the individual Hitler Youth 'is no longer alone. Wherever the banners of the Hitler Youth fly he has comrades, his brothers and sisters, united with him in one faith, one ideology, fused on one organisation. It is a marvellous and tremendous experience in which Germany's youth participates.'

The psychological impact of such a mass rally cannot be overstated. Small groups of Hitler Youths living in a state of semi-isolation, in working class districts, facing hostile parents, teachers or workmates, suddenly had

Above: The Führer greets a girl of the *Bund Deutscher Madchen* and young Hitler Youth members. *Below:* The drumbeat of nationalism. There was a measure of excitement in the activities of the Hitler Youth groups which found a universal appeal in young boys

he experience of being part of one
whole, of knowing that besides themselves there were thousands of others
in Germany all fighting for the same
aim.

At the end of the rally the youths returned tired and hungry but full of
enthusiasm and confidence in the future. One of them caught pneumonia on
an open lorry and subsequently died.
His funeral was the occasion for an
attack by their enemies.

It may be difficult to assess the influence of the Hitler Youth upon Germany's youth as a whole; certainly before 30th January 1933 the organisation failed to win over party-political-
ly associated youth groups. Within
the 'Reichs Committee of German
Youth Associations' they represented
no more than one per cent but their
indirect influence was sufficiently
persuasive for many of these youth
organisations to adapt their style and
their slogans to that of the Hitler
Youth.

The difficult years between 1926 and
1933 have been aptly summarised by
Sir Winston Churchill when he wrote:
'The story of that struggle cannot be
read without admiration for the courage, the perseverance, and the vital
force which enabled [Hitler] to challenge, defy, conciliate, or overcome,
all the authorities or resistances
which barred his path. He, and the ever
increasing legions who worked with
him, certainly at this time, in their
patriotic ardour and love of their
country, showed that there was
nothing they would not do or dare, no
sacrifice of life, limb or liberty that
they would not make themselves or
inflict upon their opponents.'

Whether, on the other hand, the
majority of the Hitler Youth members
had clear-cut ideological concepts is
more than doubtful. W S Allen in his
brilliant study, *The Nazi Seizure of
Power*, quotes a former Hitler Youth
member whose testimony may well
apply to many if not the majority of
members: 'There was no pressure put
on me by my father or anyone else to
join the Hitler Youth – I decided to
join independently simply because I
wanted to be in a boys club where I
could strive towards a nationalistic
ideal. The Hitler Youth had camping,
hikes, and group meetings. I was
number nine in the Thalburg group
when I joined in 1930. There were boys
from all classes of families though
mainly middle class and workers.
There were no social or class distinc-
tions, which I approved of very much.
There was no direct or obvious political indoctrination until later – after
Hitler came to power. Without really
trying to get new members, the Thalburg Hitler Youth grew rapidly. I
think most of the boys joined for the
same reason that I did. They were
looking for a place where they could
get together with other boys in exciting activities. It was also a depression
time and there were many evil influences abroad from which decent boys
wished to escape. In any event, I don't
think the political factor was the

Walking tall – Hitler Youth members at an open-air camp

main reason boys joined. We did march in parades and hated the SPD, but that was all general, not specific – it was all a part of it. We weren't fully conscious of what we were doing, but we enjoyed ourselves and also felt important.'

The striving towards a nationalistic ideal, not necessarily one distilled from the pages of *Mein Kampf*, and the feeling of importance were, as we shall see, two elements common to those who joined before 1933 and/or after 1939. Both groups were aware of a sense of national crisis, whether created by the aftermath of Versailles and the depression, or the fact that the country was at war. The party engendered the feeling among the youths that what they were doing was not just playing games but that they were actively participating in the struggle to restore to Germany its honour and its former position in the world.

Few of the Hitler Youths who o 30th January 1933 marched past Hitle on the evening of his appointment a Chancellor, had the remotest ide where their 'Nationalistic Ideals' an their feeling of importance would lea them within the short span of twelv years; few would even suspect to wha extent their idealism and readines for sacrifice would be exploited and t what ends. The torchlight processior of 30th January 1933, marking the be ginning of Germany's 'national revc lution', seemed to demonstrate, a least to the younger Germans, that a long last the young generation ha come into its own. None of the ol parties were ready to stand up an fight for the republic; the way it ha disappeared was symptomatic of it beginnings. The feeling of nationa renaissance transcended even Gern any's borders where, almost overnigl among the German minorities fror the Baltic countries to Transylvani supporters of Hitler took up the reir of their 'patriotic associations'.

The new spirit affected even groups of those who were ultimately to become National Socialism's most tragic victims – the German Jews. Jewish German students addressed themselves to Hitler trying to convince him of their sincere patriotism. When the liberal politician Theodor Heuss returned late in February 1933 from a meeting at which he had addressed German Jewish students, he recorded in his diary his disillusioned impression that he had spoken 'to prevented Nazis'.

Though Hitler's government was initially a coalition government, after the passing of the Enabling Act in March 1933 he had a clear road, of which the leadership of the Hitler Youth was naturally to take as much advantage as any other party formation. With the entire executive power of the state on their side, the Hitler Youth could now set about preparing its monopoly position; gradually introducing in the field of youth activities the process of *Gleichschaltung* – gradually 'coordinating' and 'integrating' all other youth movements into the Hitler Youth and forbidding other youth activity to be carried on outside it.

On 3rd April 1933 Schirach had the offices of Reichs Committee of German Youth Associations occupied. The fifty Hitler Youths who were to carry out this operation forced their way into the offices in Berlin's Alsenstrasse, but apart from office workers they could find none of its officials. Hermann Maass, who came from the youth movement of the Social Democrats and was a manager of the Committee, had to be fetched from another part of Berlin, only to be insulted by the leader of the Hitler Youth commando troop, *Obergebietsführer* Karl Nabersberg, and to be told to pack up

Hiking trip in true military style

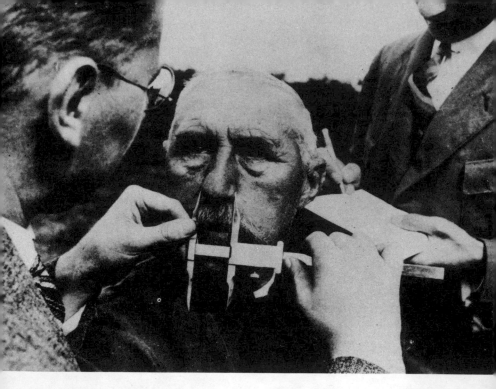

One of the ignominies of being 'of doubtful origins' – the nose measurer

his things and go home. Meanwhile, the other Hitler Youths ransacked the offices. One of them was put in charge of the office staff, but still unaccustomed to his 'authoritarian' role, he politely asked one of the clerks whether he could use their waste-paper baskets to dispose of his sandwich papers. Without putting up any resistance Maass left his office which Naberberg then occupied demanding that all employees continue their work under his direction. Schirach was now in control of the body which represented approximately 6,000,000 young Germans organised in various youth movements. The files of the Committee provided ample material for the persecution of the opponents of the Hitler Youth. It was the beginning of the *Gleichschaltung*. The first of the youth movements to be affected were the purely political ones. Already the Reichstag fire of February 1933 had provided the necessary lever to outlaw the Communist Party and any of its affiliated associations.

On the evening of the fire, leaders of radical youth movements including Hitler Youths had met in a restaurant near Berlin's Stettiner railway station. Apparently they agreed on their common social revolutionary aims and approximately 200 young men representing the revolutionary wing of the Hitler Youth, the Socialist Youth, Young Communists, Red Boyscouts, National Revolutionaries, and Otto Strasser's Black Front, promised to co-operate with one another. Among those attending were Heinz Gruber and also Harro Schulze-Boysen, later to be the leader of the Communist spy network, the *Rote Kapelle*. Many of them were beginning to see the NSDAP in a different light, as a movement of the proportions of an avalanche which was sweeping away the

May 1933 – Hitler Youth march in Berlin

Admiral von Trotha, leader of the 'Greater German League'. The league was a right-wing organization which declared its loyalty to Hitler

General Edwin von Stuelpnagel. He coordinated the *Reichswehr*'s assistance in the para-military training of German youth associations

barriers between the middle class and the proletariat. A previously vociferous opponent of the Hitler Youth wrote in a periodical: 'The trenches of the right against the left and those of the left against the right are false positions, comrades! It was a disastrous remark of the chancellor of the Centre Party when he stated "The enemy stands to the right". As disastrous as the contention that the enemy stands at the left. We oppose any attempt to tear our nation apart irrespective of whether it comes from either "left" or "right" . . . We want action against the alien influences in our nation, not merely action against "marxism".'

It is natural enough that the sudden attempts at *rapprochement* with the Hitler Youth by the left of centre parties were dictated by the changed circumstances and the fear of the demise of their own youth organisation; nevertheless there were many who believed in the validity of co-operation towards a common end.

The Reichstag fire did much to break off such attempts at *rapprochement*.

Next to the Communists, those most endangered were the 'Socialist Workers Youth of the SPD'. In some areas individual Hitler Youth units anticipated or even precipitated events. Local Headquarters of the SPD's youth movement were raided by the Hitler Youth and the files removed. Though police intervention temporarily put an end to acts of this kind, local Nazi party leaders used them as a pretext to press for the closure of a local headquarters of their opponents.

The youth movements of Hitler's 'conservative partners' within his coalition first tried to create a common front by founding the 'Greater German League' led by Admiral von Trotha. Trotha, who had retired from the German navy some time before, still enjoyed valuable contacts with the *Reichswehr* where he enjoyed the support of General Edwin von Stuelpnagel who was responsible for the *Reichswehr*'s assistance in the para-military training of German nationalist youth associations. The League explicitly excluded Jews, Democrats and Socialists from its membership.

New and old in confrontation; Hitler shakes hands with the medal-bedecked Hindenburg

It issued a proclamation expressing loyalty to Hitler and to the National Socialist state, and for a short time managed to convey the impression of being able to overtake the Hitler Youth on the Right. The March elections, though they failed to provide Hitler with an absolute majority, combined with the Enabling Act, quickly turned the coalition government into Hitler's personal dictatorship and his cabinet colleagues were quick to see the warning lights. They immediately joined the party and took steps to fuse their own paramilitary organisations and youth movements with those of the NSDAP. This in essence was the end of 'Greater German League' although it was allowed to linger on for a few more months. By controlling the Reichs Committee, the Hitler Youth in effect controlled the whole of Germany's organised youth, and those who, like their elders, could read the sign of the times, joined its ranks. Within the League itself suggestions were made of joining the Hitler youth en bloc. Both Schirach and Hitler opposed this

measure for tactical reasons, for it would have meant that all the other previously non-NSDAP youth movements would have joined together with their leaders, and consequently create a body of serious opposition within the Hitler Youth. At Whitsun 1933 the League held its last camp meeting only to be sent home by police and stormtrooper contingents on Whit Monday. A month later the League 'officially' dissolved itself, which did not prevent Trotha from raising an official protest and carrying it as far as Hindenburg. But nothing came of the protest and even the Admiral reconciled himself with the existing situation by accepting from Schirach the appointment as 'Honorary Leader of the Marine Hitler Youth'. The Reichs Committee had served its function too and was dissolved on 8th July. Seven days before, Schirach had passed new measures for the regional organisation of the Hitler

Hitler Youth membership (males and females aged 10–18)

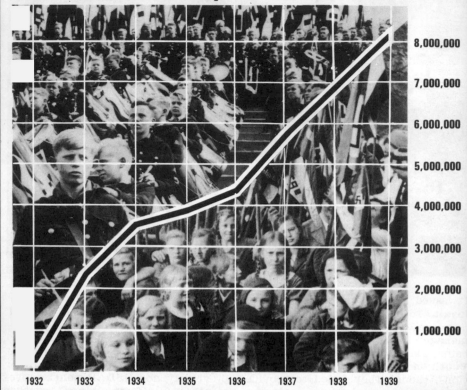

Hitler Youth membership 1932-1939

Youth as well as for the introduction of structure based on age groups which was to remain in force until 1945.

With the dissolution of the Reichs Committee, the *Reichsjugendführer*, was now, in effect, the sole authority of state-organised youth movements. The transition from a party youth movement to the 'German State Youth' was beginning, since his function was now national as well as party political, and his position was at one and the same time that of civil servant and that of a party functionary. Besides his party title of *Reichsjugendführer*, Schirach now also carried the title of *Jugendführer des Deutschen Reiches* – Youth Leader of the German Reich. It did not give him entire control of youth affairs in Germany. The Ministry of the Interior as well as the Ministry of Justice and the newly created Ministry for Science and Education all participated through their own administrative agencies, such as youth welfare, in deciding youth policy. The net result was a proliferation of responsibility. The only certainty inherent in the system was a continuous conflict of temperament and authority which was to lead directly to the assumption of power by the strongest single element: Adolf Hitler.

While the political integration or suppression of youth movements not allied to any party was achieved relatively easily, the organised youth of the Protestant and Roman Catholic denominations appeared at first to present a more formidable problem. Again it was the Protestant Youth movements that were most easily won over. The appeal made to them was simple and effective: 'A new hour in Germany's history is striking. In the last second Germany has been pulled back from the abyss of Bolshevism. A strong government calls upon all Germans to realise their responsibility. A new movement breaks a path which promises to bridge the differences between classes, estates and ethnic groups.'

And they responded in a similar vein: 'In this hour Germany's evangelic Youth ought to know that its leaders answer a joyous 'Yes' to the rising of the nation. The recognition that that which is at stake is the rejuvenation of the foundations of the life of the entire race and that this lies at the very core of the historical mission of the evangelic youth, it calls for the ready sacrifice of earthly goods and blood.' With these words one of the leading Protestant Youth leaders – Erich Stange – greeted the Third Reich and Protestant clergymen were the authors of some of the most pathetic Hitler-adulating poems.

Within the Catholic Youth movement, developments took a different turn. In his government proclamation of 23rd March 1933 Hitler promised his support for the Christian churches, and the continuation of the Concordats which individual German regions had made with the Vatican. Moreover, the news was soon leaked that the German government had sent Vice Chancellor von Papen to Rome to negotiate a new Concordat for the whole of Germany. This was successfully concluded and what Hitler did not obtain through the front door he managed to get through the back. The Roman Catholic episcopacy withdrew its traditional political support for the Centre Party. But the unreserved adulation which Hitler received from the Protestant Youth community was not shown by the majority of Catholics. Their youth movements felt the threat of the Hitler Youth as did most other non-Nazi youth organisations, but as a result of the Concordat they felt that they had been given a new lease of life, which their bishops defended with vigilance.

However, Roman Catholics and National Socialists – and it must not be forgotten that many a Nazi party member was also a practising Catholic – shared a good deal besides opposition to Versailles and the establishment of

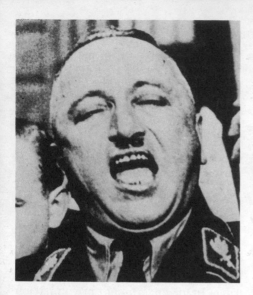

Dr Robert Ley, leader of the German Labour Front, a Nazi substitute for the dissolved trade unions

Grossdeutschland. Both felt a revulsion against the divisions of the 'party-state' of Weimar, rejected the principles of liberalism, and believed in the creation of an 'organically developed' German nation based on the principle of the corporate state.

By late summer 1933, with the exception of the denominational organisations, all youth movements had been compulsorily integrated or 'co-ordinated'. Hitler's first objective had been attained. The Communist and Socialist Youth groups had been dissolved and declared illegal and the other youth groups had either 'voluntarily' dissolved themselves or joined the formations of the Hitler Youth.

But inter-party rivalries within the NSDAP affected the Hitler Youth. The *Reichssport* leader, Hans von Tschammer und Osten, endeavoured to keep control of the organised *Sportsjugend* and keep it remote from Schirach's interference. Robert Ley, the leader of the *Deutsche Arbeits-Front,* the German Labour Front, a Nazi substitute for the dissolved trade unions, pursued much the same

aims with the working youth, who automatically upon entering employment had to become members of the DAF. These two specific rivalries were not to be resolved until 1936 when Schirach got his own way, but they were not by any means the only ones. The *Reichswehr,* renamed the *Wehrmacht* in 1935 wished to exercise a controlling influence upon the Hitler Youth which, though only mainly in order to appease the conservative forces, Hitler was ready to grant. This influence was rivalled in the two years before the war, and increasingly and more successfully during it, by that of the SS, especially the *SS-Verfügungtruppen* later to be known as the *Waffen-SS.*

In face of these rivalries, dealing with the denominational youth groups seemed to be a more immediately soluble problem. Again regional Hitler Youth leaders took the law into their own hands by issuing decrees forbidding assemblies of youth movements other than those of the Hitler Youth. By the extent of the liberties taken, Schirach was compelled to issue the following order on 5th July 1933: 'I hereby forbid any interference by members of the Hitler Youth with other youth associations. If the behaviour of members of other youth associations gives cause for complaint then the complaint is to be directed to me through the official channels. Insofar as the complaints necessitate further action I shall initiate the necessary steps through the appropriate state institutions. Individual actions will be punished.'

In order to preserve their autonomy, various Protestant Youth groups were prepared to cooperate with the Hitler Youth at a regional level by joint meetings, public rallies, and leadership gatherings. But the bridge thus built carried only a one-way traffic to the Hitler Youth. Moreover,

Dr Ley at the opening of the Adolf Hitler school for members of the Hitler Youth at Kroessinsee

the rank and file of the members were betrayed by their own leaders when they accepted the subordination of the Protestant Youth Movements under *Reichsbisdrof* Ludwig Mueller.

Mueller had been a divisional chaplain at the Dardanelles during the First World War and after that the army district of East Prussia was under his 'spiritual' care. An early convert to Nazism, he was responsible for the conversion of Colonel von Reichenau and through him of Reichenau's chief, General von Blomberg. Both met Hitler in Mueller's house. After 30th January 1933 Hitler appointed Mueller 'Plenipotentiary of the Chancellor in Questions of the Evangelical Church' and through him Hitler hoped to create an indigenous 'German Church for German Christians'.

Mueller, of course was in favour of fusing the youth movements of his church with the Hitler Youth, but found opposition among his colleagues such as Pastor Niemoeller, but more especially from the ranks of many of the youth leaders themselves. Mueller could always point to the example provided by the Protestant Youth of Danzig which, on its own initiative, had joined the Hitler Youth.

Divided internally, the Protestant church was forced ultimately to give way to the concerted pressure of the Hitler Youth and the NSDAP and on 19th December 1933 an agreement was signed according to which the Protestant Youth movements accepted uniform political instruction by the National Socialist State and the HJ. All members under the age of eighteen were to be integrated into the Hitler Youth and its sub-organisations. The only concession made to the Protestant Youth was that two afternoons a week should remain free for the educational activity of the church, a

Bishop Mueller, an early convert to Nazism. Through him Hitler hoped to create an indigenous 'German Church for German Christians'

concession quickly eroded by excess demands on the boys and girls which took up their entire time and limited religious instruction exclusively to the home and to one hour per week in the schools. The agreement was met by a wave of protest but they were powerless to undo what had been done.

The Reichs Concordat concluded between the Vatican and the German Reich on 20th July 1933 gave the Catholic Youth movements a little more breathing space. But one of its provisions left a loophole which the NSDAP was quick to exploit. Article 31 stated that those catholic organisations and associations whose purpose was exclusively religious or cultural would enjoy the full protection of their establishments and activities. But this was followed by a limiting clause that the determination of organisations and associations which were subject to that article would be subject to bilateral agreement between the government of the Reich and Roman Catholic Episcopacy.

Years of negotiations between party and Hitler Youth leaders on the one hand and Catholic bishops on the other went on to determine precisely this, with each party accusing the other of breaking the Concordat. Of course there is no doubt that the National Socialist State, determined to be the sole educator of its youth, was bent upon breaking the Concordat before it was even signed. The defensive position of the Catholic Church was stronger only because it was, after all, a universal organisation with a strongly hierarchical structure which did not allow dissenting opinions within to affect its attitude towards the world without.

Cardinal Bertram, the Bishop of Breslau, first asked the question, 'which functions could the Catholic Church and its youth organisations hand over to the National Socialist State?' His conclusion was essentially negative: hiking, sports and similar physical activities as modern means of education were, he argued, as

Cardinal Bertram, Bishop of Breslau. He believed that the Nazi youth organizations could take over some of the minor functions of the Catholic Church, such as the organization of physical activities

Adolf Wagner, Gauleiter of Upper Bavaria. He was fiercely anti-clerical and saw the Catholic Church in particular as another form of Judaic conspiracy against the German *Volk*

**Propaganda bicycle ride in Berlin.
Every form of parade was undertaken
– to recruit new members and
demonstrate solidarity**

important for practical Christianity
as were the Rosary and other purely
religious exercises. Conflict soon en-
sued.

The anticlerical wing of the Nazi
party was headed by Alfred Rosenberg
and Julius Streicher and numerous
Gauleiters, like Adolf Wagner of Upper
Bavaria who looked at Christianity
in general, and Roman Catholicism in
particular, as another form of Judaic
conspiracy against the German *Volk*,
whose most dangerous executive
organ was the Jesuits. On a purely
legal level the fight was conducted by
the Nazis on the basis of pretexts.
Catholic journals were compelled
to cease publication because they
had printed allegedly subversive
articles. Youth organisations were
closed down because of infringement
of the currency laws. The public

rallies of the Catholic Youth were
forbidden, and when a member of the
Hitler Youth committed suicide a
press campaign was mounted arguing
that he had been driven to take this
step by a Catholic conspiracy. Like
many of the Protestant Youth leaders,
some Catholic Youth leaders were at
first under the illusion that the persecution was simply the result of a
serious misunderstanding which
could be easily cleared up by co-
operating with the Hitler Youth.
But they were never meant to be
given a chance and they had none.
No agreement such as that between
the Hitler Youth and the Protestant
church came about, while the law
enacted in 1936 making service in the
Hitler Youth compulsory, also prac-
tically put an end to the organised
Catholic Youth.

1933 had brought rapid growth within the ranks of the Hitler Youth,
which, however, lacked one thing –
an effective leadership adequate to
cope with the numbers. As a result,

many former leaders of other youth movements managed to acquire important positions, which was precisely what Schirach had feared. In Hesse, for instance, numerous instances became known of former trade union leaders and socialists becoming, on the surface at least, Hitler Youth leaders and who under this guise endeavoured to keep together a cadre of the youths they had led before 1933.

To provide leaders orientated along National Socialist principles and in sufficient quantity, a *Reichsführer* school was founded in Potsdam in 1933, an example emulated in every other German province. Schirach, enmeshed in the intrigues of internal rivalries within the party, realised that note would be made of every shortcoming of the organisation under his command, that the Hitler Youth would stand or fall by the quality of his leadership. In 1934 he created the precedent which was to be followed every subsequent year up to 1939, that of putting each year's activities under a particular heading which then became the annual slogan. 1934 was entitled 'The Year of Training', in which Hitler Youth leaders were to be produced en masse. It was to provide the leaders with 'sound' historic, political and racial knowledge as well as extensive physical training. Schirach emphasised that 'the Hitler Youth is a community of ideological education. Whoever marches in the Hitler Youth is not a number among millions but the soldier of an idea. The individual member's value to the whole is determined by the degree with which he is permeated by the idea. The best Hitler Youth, irrespective of rank and office, is he who completely surrenders himself to the National Socialist *Weltanschauung*.'

On 24th January 1934, the birthday of Frederick the Great and the second anniversary of the death of Herbert Norkus, a mass rally took place at Potsdam. Three hundred and forty-two Hitler Youth colours were handed over to HJ units. By the end of Febru-ary Schirach had made his peace with Ley and both Schirach and Ley called for a *Reichs* competition, in which the best performances of Hitler Youths in their respective occupations were assessed. The victors were personally received by Hitler. Increasingly, the year could be divided into specific Nazi holidays, one of them, 7th June, was 'The Day of the State's Youth'. For Hitler Youths still at school Saturday lessons were cancelled to allow the whole day to be used for physical and para-military training. During the early years the latter were frequently conducted with tear gas grenades and pistols firing blanks.

For the girls a total of twenty-seven 'leader' schools were founded during the first half of 1934, but most of them bore the hallmarks of improvisation. Much the same, of course, applied to their male equivalents. Still, in August 1934 Schirach could submit an official report claiming to have produced in 287 three-week-courses 12,727 HJ leaders and 24,660 *Jungvolk* leaders. 15,000 Hitler Youth leaders had passed special physical exercise training courses. Indeed it was a proud day for many of the youngsters, of which the particular sequence in Leni Riefenstahl's film 'Triumph of the Will', bears eloquent witness when Hitler, flanked by Schirach and Goebbels, addressed them at the Nuremberg party rally, calling them the guarantors of the future behind which 'one day the entire German nation will march'. By that time Schirach, thanks to Hitler's support had overcome all internal opposition. All youth groups, of the party and outside it with the exception of the Catholics, had been 'coordinated.'

The Hitler Youth obtained its own broadcasting time over the *Deutsch-landsender* and a special Hitler Youth institute was created to train its employees in the use of the microphone. In German grammar schools it had been customary to wear special caps, usually a sign of class distinction. In a public ceremony they were

Women, too, were encouraged to practice sports and to keep fit. Here, a women's javelin team line up at a Berlin sports meeting

Female gymnasts at the *Reichs* competition organized by Robert Ley. The victors in each event were personally received by Hitler

A still from Leni Riefenstahl's film,
Triumph of the Will, made during the
Party rally at Nuremberg in 1934

banned from all schools and burned by Hitler Youths in all German cities. Schoolteachers judged to be supporters of the new 'classless' state were publicly honoured and schools in which ninety per cent of the pupils were Hitler Youth members were awarded a Hitler Youth banner.

The so-called 'Röhm-putsch' too had favourable results upon the Hitler Youth. Legally up to that time it had always been subordinate to the stormtroopers. After 30th June 1934 the Hitler Youth, like the SS gained its autonomy *de facto*. On 9th November 1934, the anniversary of the Munich putsch of 1923, at which eighteen-year old Hitler Youths were normally transferred into the ranks of the stormtroopers, no such transfer took place. Instead they became members of the NSDAP. On 29th March 1935 this change was legally registered by an executive order which listed the Hitler Youth next to the SA and SS and other organisations as a subordinate branch of the NSDAP.

1934 also saw the introduction into the Hitler Youth of a body exercising policing functions – the *HJ-Streifendienst* – comparable in its context perhaps with the military police whose function it was to see that 'law and order' were upheld within the ranks and to combat any illegal opposition. In its operations the *Streifendienst* closely cooperated with the SS and the Gestapo, a relationship formalised four years later between Himmler and Schirach in an agreement which described its functions and responsibilities within the Hitler Youth as being identical with those which the SS carried for the whole of the *Reich*. The *Streifendienst* was also to serve as a special reservoir for SS recruits, the *SS Totenkopfverbände* ('Death's Head' Units responsible for guarding the concentration camps) and the '*Junkerschulen*' the SS-Officers' schools. The highly confidential 'Information Service' distributed among the upper ranks of the Hitler Youth during the prewar years shows not merely that the *Streifendienst* was a highly effective organisation in its detection of opposition, but also that in spite of suppression and the *Gleichschaltung* opposition within the Hitler Youth to official policy time and again reared its head.

While 1935 was the year dedicated to physical training, the year 1936 was 'The Year of the German *Jungvolk*', of those between ten and fourteen years of age. A vast campaign was initiated to recruit as many boys as possible. The aim was that the entire age group born in 1926, boys and girls, should 'volunteer' to join the *Jungvolk* by 20th April as a birthday present for Hitler's forty-seventh birthday. In order to carry out the recruitment drive as successfully as possible, the Hitler Youth adapted itself to the NSDAP district division (Ortsgruppe) which came after the cell, and the block division. Within one such district approximately 150 ten to fourteen year-olds lived organised in the *Fähnlein* (squad) approximately 150-strong, or of company strength. Girls were organised according to the same pattern. These units within their district carried out extensive recruitment campaigns, marches, evenings of choir singing, and parents' evenings. Teachers of primary and secondary schools, who by that time in order to stay in the profession had been compelled to join if not the party then at least the *Reichslehrerbund*, were persuaded to make their pupils join the *Jungvolk*. The recruitment drive reached its highest pitch during the last four weeks preceding Hitler's birthday.

The place for the official celebration was the *Marienburg*, the Castle of the Teutonic Order, which was chosen as the political example worth the emulation of every Hitler Youth. There, in the gothic main hall among the light of candles and torchlights, the new members of the *Jungvolk* swore the oath that was to be repeated every 20th April, including that of 1945.

Above: Blonde eight-year-olds, reared on nationalism, give the Nazi salute.
Below: Hitler heads a march celebrating the 1923 Munich putsch

Camp games. Hitler proposed that as a forty-seventh birthday present to himself all boys and girls born in 1926 should 'volunteer' to join the *Jungvolk*

'I promise
In the Hitler Youth
to do my duty
at all times
In love and faithfulness
to the Führer
So help me God.

And then followed fifes, drums and fanfares and the Hitler Youth anthem '*Vorwärts, vorwärts, schmettern die hellen Fanfaren, vorwärts, vorwärts,*

Jugend kennt keine Gefahre' (Forward forward sound the fanfares, forward forward, youth knows no dangers) From then on boys and girls were on probation for between two and six months. This period was concluded with a special test, combining sport, close combat, and questions of an 'ideological' nature (mainly a knowledge of the history of the NSDAP) and culminating in a 'test of bravery' which (as in the author's case) could take the form of having to jump in full dress and boots from the window of a first floor block of flats. After passing the test, the *Jungvolk* member

was entitled to wear the 'scout' knife, but shaped in the form of a military bayonet, though of course smaller, the shoulder strap and the *Jungvolk* insignias on the brown shirt. Every *Ortsgruppe*, every district, now had one *Fähnlein* each of the HJ, the *Jungvolk*, the Young Girl's League and the BDM.

Finally on 1st December 1936 came the step which had been expected for a long time, the law by which the government made membership of the Hitler Youth compulsory from the age of ten onwards, and by which the task of 'educating the entire German youth in the Hitler Youth' was given to the *Reichsjugendführer* of the NSDAP, Baldur von Schirach. His position was defined as a governmental one with its centre in Berlin and responsible directly to 'the Führer and Chancellor'. With parental and school education, the Hitler Youth had now become the third important legal force shaping and moulding the character of Germany's youth.

komm lieber Mai und ma

Blood and soil

'Racial teaching is the point of departure of all National Socialist teaching, from it the consequences of National Socialist youth education derive. Corresponding with the will of the Führer the strengthening and toughening of one's physical capacity is the first as well as the highest duty of the young generation. In order to measure physical strength, continuous struggle is required, a struggle which alone will produce the racially fittest to survive. Self-confidence obtained through struggle and victory must be acquired by every member of the [German] racial community from the earliest days of his childhood. His entire education must be planned with the aim of giving him the conviction of superiority over others. The young must accustom themselves at an early stage to acknowledge the superiority of the stronger and to subordinate himself to him . . . '

This dubious intellectual exercise, contained in a PhD thesis of 1940, fused a vulgar version of social Darwinism with racialism, and it reflects adequately what in many quarters of the Hitler Youth and NSDAP leadership was described as 'ideology'. The question is to what extent was it actually possible within the space of twelve years (only seven of which fully embraced the entire German youth within the ranks of the Hitler Youth) for this 'ideology' to penetrate the minds of all the members? And this raises the fundamental problems as to what extent National Socialist Germany was actually a fully totalitarian state, capable of enforcing its will and ideas upon every single member of the national community.

As an 'ideology' National Socialism as propounded by Hitler was a hotch potch in no way comparable with the systematic theoretical structure of

'Come dear May, and make us free from the Jews' — anti-semitic slogans in Berlin at a time of economic depression

Structural organisation of the Hitler Youth in 1942

A song book cover displays the emblems of nationalism and socialism

Marxist/Leninism. From Hitler's as well as from Himmler's point of view the one 'ideological' tenet in which National Socialism was consistent was its anti-semitism. However, this was not a tenet around which it would have been possible to rally a mass party, only at most a lunatic fringe movement. Consequently, in order to popularise anti-semitism as a cause it had to be identified with the political and economic ills of the time. The prominence of some Jewish-Soviet leaders in Russia or in the Communist and Socialist parties allowed the creation of a conspiracy theory whereby 'international Jewry' was about to enslave the German people through 'Soviet tyranny'. But even more effective at a time of an economic depression only six years after the end of the inflation which had effectively brought the German lower middle class near a state of proletarization, was the appeal to an economically motivated anti-semitism, which was inevitably bound to create a greater response than a racially formulated abstract one. The 'Money Power of the Banks', the impact of industrialization favouring big business and pushing the artisan, the small trader, against the wall, the depersonalization of an industrial society – all that could be blamed on 'international financiers' and the fact that some of them were indeed Jews; to minds incapable of explaining to themselves the complexity of industrial change and the consequences involved, an 'international Jewish conspiracy' provided a plausible enough explanation. Anti-semitism then, based on economic grievances rather than on racial grounds was a facet of the Nazi platform to which the masses responded. The Nazi formula of 'blood and soil' the interdependence of the racial stock linked to the purity and yield of the soil was nothing other than a derivative of the slogan created by Barres after 1870 'la terre et les morts'. It was a racialist slogan which, like the economically motivated anti-semitism, appealed to a society which had not yet fully come to terms with an industrial environment, to a generation which looked back to the 'golden days gone by'. Hitler's emphasis on the creation of a true *Volksgemeinschaft* (a truly German national community) appealed to traditions which went back at least as far as the days of the Wars of Liberation against Napoleon, only to be frustrated by the forces of dynastic reaction after 1815. Hence Bismarck's Germany was to many Germans not the completion of the German national state but only a halfway house towards it. Hitler promised to complete Bismarck's work, and indeed, for a very short time, he did.

But for Hitler to introduce successfully a completely totalitarian state he would have had to destroy the traditional social ties of the people, as the Bolsheviks had done in 1917. Instead, he posed as their stout defender, which brought him the support from even the ultra-conservative camp, knowing that he needed the support of the traditional powers to pursue his policy successfully, but at the same time he could begin to plant the germinal cells for a fully totalitarian state of the future. For the time being, the old institutions coexisted with those of the party, and increasingly so during the latter years of the war. Germany was now a totalitarian state which embraced every single member of the state, and forced every citizen into the political process, but which still allowed the existence of considerable areas of 'political privacy'. In other words, if one detested the methods of Hitler and his party but was not prepared actively to oppose him it was still possible to opt out of politics altogether. Nazi totalitarianism never reached the point where it could penetrate into the innermost recesses of every individual's life, making every single action, private and public, subject to judgment according

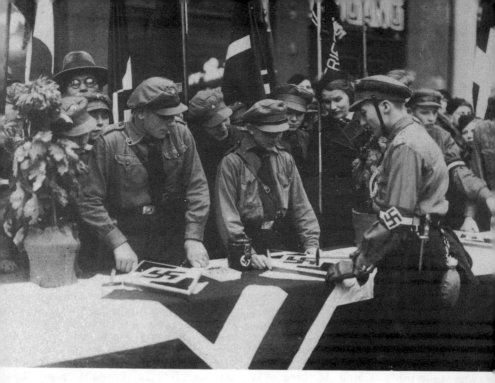

Hitler Youths organize a Winter Aid collection

to the criteria of National Socialist ideology. During the full twelve years of Hitler's rule such ideological coherence was never attained.

Any systematic study of the official publications for the use of the Hitler Youth reveals how little space was given to actual politico-ideological writings. Most prominent are reproductions of Hitler's utterances in stylised gothic lettering and detailed reports about Hitler Youth activities in other parts of the country.

Looking at the institutional position of the Hitler Youth within the Nazi party apparatus the impression can easily be gained that it was a rigid body which left little room for spontaneity and autonomous development. This may well be true of the *Reichsjugendführung's* position vis à vis the NSDAP, but at a lower level where youth was in fact led by youth the picture was a different one. The average age of a *Bannführer* was twenty-four, an age drastically reduced after the outbreak of war. A *Gefolgschaftsführer* was rarely older than seventeen, a *Faehnleinsführer* in the *Jungvolk* between fourteen and fifteen. By 1945 a *Jungzugführer*, responsible for a unit of approximately fifty boys, could be just over eleven years old (as in the case of the author).

Consequently, never before or since in German history did youth occupy such positions of power, never before did any single one of their actions seem of almost national importance – one inevitable by-product being the arrogance with which many Hitler Youths tended to look down on the older generation. The continuous emphasis upon action, whether propaganda marches, sports competitions or Winter Aid collections, left very little room or time for thought, for systematic ideological indoctrination. This applies to an even greater degree to the war years when from its outbreak HJ, *Jungvolk*, BDM and *Jungmädels* became more and more involved at the home-front, until finally many of them stood in the front line themselves, already more familiar with death than with the 'facts of life'.

The image of millions of little Hitler Youths studying or learning by heart Hitler's *Mein Kampf* is one derived from fiction and not from reality. What was found too indigestible at *SS-Junker* schools was bound to have the same effect among younger age groups. Such ideological tenets, if one can call them that, as nationalism and the belief in the moral and physical superiority of one's own country were not specifically National Socialist but could have been found in any moderate Right-wing party before 1933.

One ideological tenet put into practice on a large scale was the bridging of the class conflict. At no time was the problem of 'class conflict' ever analysed or subjected to theoretical discussion but instead it was dismissed as one of the excesses of a degenerate democracy. The determining factor was now the 'leadership principle'; workers and employers marched behind the same flag in the same uniform for the same aim. The intellectual and the peasant were now working for a common aim – for the good of the national community. Within the ranks of the Hitler Youth social barriers were broken down, the entire educational system was geared to further a particular brand of egalitarianism, in which wealth did not predetermine the availability of opportunities. Schools designed to produce an élite did exist, but these were not private schools, but NS schools in which the cost was relatively low. There were of course . . . isolated instances of 'separatism' as for instance . . . during the war years, when boys of an upper middle class district in Munich formed their own little clique within a Hitler Youth unit, separate from those who lived in a working class district or members who did not attend grammar school. The intervention of the authorities was as drastic as it was effective. The boys concerned were 'sent to Coventry' and for three months had to devote their entire spare time to carrying out chores for working class families. After three months the cure had proved its value and within the unit concerned everything returned to normal as though nothing had happened. The Allied bombing offensive drove home more than ever the realisation of the need of *Kameradschaft*, the unhesitating reliability upon one another.

One of the main reasons why the 'National Socialist ideology' did not meet many receptive minds was its lack of a systematic doctrined body. Ideology was often replaced by a confused 'party historical mythology' with an emphasis on the 'blood witnesses' of the Nazi movement, like the sixteen dead of the Munich putsch of 1923, and of course Horst Wessel and Herbert Norkus. From the younger age groups of *Jungvolk* to the older ones of the HJ, most Hitler Youth publications were taken for what they were, rather clumsy propaganda.

Indirect ideological influence was exerted through the 'coordinated' mass media such as the press, films and theatres, but the absence of effective sources of propaganda was a shortcoming realised during the last few years of the war when the *Reichsjugendführung* introduced a 'HJ-Catechism' which, in turn, appears to have been received with indifference. A check on supplies of the book in Hitler Youth headquarters in Berlin, Munich, Hamburg, Dresden, Essen, Dusseldorf, Breslau and Koenigberg showed that the stocks delivered had not even been collected. Besides, members of the Hitler Youth frequently expressed the opinion that they were kept far too busy anyway to have time for concentrated reading.

The Reich Concordat of 1933 seemed to have determined the relationship between the Nazi régime and Roman Catholic Church. But, as already

Occupations of the Hitler Youth in 1939

Industrial and manual workers
42%

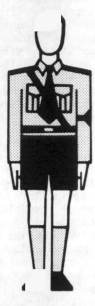

Occupation in agriculture and forestry
23%

Pupils
21%

Commercial occupations
5%

Technicians
3%

Others
6%

Occupations of the Hitler Youth leaders in 1937

Commercial occupations
25.5%

Pupils
16.4%

Technicians
8.7%

Students
5.9%

Teachers
5.4%

Occupation in agriculture and forestry
3.5%

Others
13.8%

indicated, the truce was short-lived and virtually open warfare between church and state broke out again soon afterwards. Officially Hitler chose to ignore the churches as long as they did not directly interfere with his actions. If they stepped on forbidden territory, the nature of his response depended upon circumstances. When, for instance, during the first few years of the war the implementation of his euthanasia programme became public knowledge and catholic and protestant clergymen spoke out against it, he agreed to have it stopped. At a time of national crisis he could not afford to alienate the churches. But before the war and also during a large part of it the *Gauleiters* of the NSDAP lived an almost autonomous existence. Hence the relationship between the NSDAP as well as the Hitler Youth depended very much on the attitudes of the local *Gauleiter*, but even the *Gauleiter*'s power of action within his regions had its limits. When in 1940 *Gauleiter* Adolf Wagner of Upper Bavaria ordered the removal of all crucifixes from schoolrooms, the public outcry of a traditionally Roman Catholic province was such that, for reasons of expediency, he had to be replaced by *Gauleiter* Giesler.

In the years between 1933 and 1937 individual party leaders could assume a greater degree of militancy against the churches than at a later date. The Bishop of Münster, Count Galen, for instance, had a considerable record of denunciations against the shortcomings of the Weimar Republic and shortly after Hitler had come to power he asked his congregation to co-operate with the new régime in order to restore Germany to her 'rightful position' among the nations. But he made a clear distinction between Hitler and the chief advocate of 'neo-heathendom' Alfred Rosenberg. When in 1935 the news came that

Horst Wessel at the Party Day Rally at Nuremberg in 1929

Above: The funeral of Horst Wessel – killed in a brawl and designated martyr by the NSDAP. *Below:* The face of the Church in sympathy – Count Galen, Bishop of Münster. He encouraged his flock to cooperate with the new regime in order to restore Germany to her 'rightful position' among the nations of the world

Rosenberg was to address a public rally in Münster he immediately addressed a letter of protest to the *Gauleiter* of Westphalia stating categorically 'That the overwhelming Christian population of Westphalia could regard the appearance of Rosenberg only as an outright provocation, designed to pour contempt on their holiest and most cherished religious convictions.'

Nevertheless Rosenberg did come on 7th July, and the local party administration turned the occasion into an ostentatious rally held in Münster's main square which also happened to be the place of the Bishop's residence. Count Galen was denounced as epitomising the forces of reaction and Frick, Minister of the Interior, whom Rosenberg, against the former's original inclinations, had persuaded to attend, made a speech on the separation of church and state. Rosenberg's speech inevitably carried metaphysical undertones; while advocating 'Germanic Spiritual Freedom', he argued the case against the superstition inherent in Christianity but could find no other solution than to replace it with the superstition inherent in his Germanic racial blood-thinking. Towards the end of his speech he turned to attack Bishop Count Galen, asking him personally whether the National Socialist party had done more to overcome the 'Bolshevik menace' than any other political force. He asserted that religious toleration was one of the basic constituents of government policy illustrating this 'toleration' by the example of the bishop himself who had written letters defamatory to Rosenberg and could do so without risk of imprisonment.

The meeting ended with Hitler Youth formations marching up in front of the Bishop's residence and chanting personally insulting as well as anti-clerical slogans. Formations of Hitler Youths were used for similar demonstrations against the Bishop of Trier and the Archbishop of Paderborn; but in all three cases the Hitler Youths had been specially 'imported' from other German regions. Hitler Youths were used for purposes of a similar kind in other parts of Germany also, but whether these young boys were genuinely motivated by the new ideology is doubtful. It seems more likely that the parades and marches merely gave vent to their excess energies, and that the idea of a free ride to a different part of Germany, a plentiful supply of food and several days off from either school or work appealed to them on a very basic level.

Now and then attempts were made, especially among Hitler Youth leaders, to persuade them to leave the church. One German historian records his own experience as a Hitler Youth: 'Our headmaster was a National Socialist, an "old fighter" who, soon after Hitler's seizure of power, was given his chance. He was no one's favourite, but nor was he hated. He was considered as somewhat thick-headed but well meaning. He was one of the many who in those days made small careers for themselves. One day – I was a sixth-former – he stopped me and asked, "You are a Hitler Youth leader, how is it that you are still attending Catholic religious instruction?" I personally did not like attending religious instruction because I found it boring. But I was angry at being approached in this way and therefore replied, "Sir, it so happens that I am a Catholic and intend to remain one." He said, "You are right. One should always remain faithful to one's convictions." He was typical of the National Socialists, of a bourgeois brand who wanted to dispell any suspicion of personal opportunism and who in the continued existence of the churches found their moral alibi.'

Schirach clearly disassociated himself from the extreme anti-Christian wing within the NSDAP when he said, 'It is my purpose neither to reerect in the forests of Germany heathen altars and introduce youth to any kind of Woden's cult, nor in any other way to hand over young Germany to the magical arts of any herb-apostles . . . I promise the German public that the youth of the German Reich, the youth of Adolf Hitler will fulfil their duty in the spirit of Adolf Hitler, to whom alone their lives belong.'

It has frequently been argued that the imagination of the young was caught by teutonic ceremonies and rituals which were allegedly widely practiced. Moreover, it is often said that ideological indoctrination was particularly effective and carried out by highly skilled instructors familiar with the entire range of techniques of ideological persuasion. This range included the pulsating rhythm of the marching columns and the united singing of Nazi songs endlessly repeated. Each boy and girl was introduced into the collective experience which dissolved their individuality

and unified them with their comrades. However, it is impossible to substantiate accounts of this kind. As far as the last point is concerned any organised camp experience produces to a greater or lesser extent that result. It would hardly be skilful to keep up indoctrination by the endless repetition of Nazi songs, and when one looks at a Hitler Youth song book one is surprised at just how few of the songs were actually of Nazi origin. The main body of songs was derived from those of the pre-1914 German youth movement, which in turn had adapted many of the songs and ballads of traditional German folklore. Some of these were of an anti-clerical nature. Thus at his interrogation at the Nuremberg trials Schirach was accused of having specially anti-clerical songs composed and written for the Hitler Youth such as '*Wir sind des Geyer's schwarzer Haufen. . . *' (We are the Geyer's black band . . .) Schirach could validly point out that the song in question had been sung in

Hitler poses with young boys and girls in the year war was declared

Germany for centuries primarily in Protestant areas, and that it originated from the 16th century Peasants' Revolt aimed at the landowning aristocracy and the rich monastries.

To teach the Hitler Youth to despise their Christian heritage and to denigrate clergymen as traitors to their own country, would hardly have been the operation of a 'skilled instructor' who must have been aware of the important role family life still played and of the important influence of the church.

The National Socialist régime had to tread carefully in its relations with the church before the war. The extravagances of individual Nazi leaders pursuing their own anti-clerical campaigns could prove rather embarrassing and it was on Hitler's own explicit orders that fabricated show trials of priests because of sexual or currency offences were

Heinrich Himmler meets the Führer
at the Berghof in the Bavarian
mountains

stopped. As yet the time had not
come when Hitler could afford to fall
out with the church. And even less so
once the war had begun. Though in
his 'Table Talk' he raged against the
church, the prophesies he made refer
to what he would do with it once the
war was over. While the war lasted the
most he required was its tacit acqui-
escence to his rule and even that at
times, as over the question of euthanasia, could not be obtained.

The war also made a considerable
difference to the catholic as well as

to some protestant youth groups still
in existence underground. In one
Munich diocese such a group voluntarily dissolved itself in order to play
an active part in the Hitler Youth.
Youngsters now realised that the
struggle of religion against Nazi
extremism had been superseded by
the 'cause of the Fatherland against
its enemies'. It was quite a common
feature in Munich churches to see on
Sundays at mass, complete Hitler
Youth units in uniform among the
congregation, and a Hitler Youth as
the altar servant.

Had the ideological permeation of
Germany's youth and its anti-Christian indoctrination between 1933 and

94

1945 been as thorough and perfect as has frequently been suggested one wonders why the Nazi creed was so quickly shed by the majority the moment Nazi Germany had collapsed. One explanation, or part of a much more complex one, is that this creed in most cases was merely a veneer that could be quickly discarded when circumstances allowed.

However, it is beyond all doubt that National Socialist ideology – as seen by Hitler, Himmler or Rosenberg – was intrinsically anti-Christian, that in the long term a direct confrontation between Hitler's Germany and the Christian Churches would have been inevitable. Furthermore, it lay

in the interest of this 'ideology' to have its youth removed from all Christian influences; in a minority of cases it can even be said that it succeeded. But generally speaking, Hitler's attitude to the churches was determined by tactical considerations and these often required the making of – in his view temporary – concessions to the religious denominations. The Roman Catholic church never abandoned its claim upon the spiritual education of Germany's youth; Hitler could at most erect obstacles but never explicitly support or advocate an anti-Christian education of the youth that marched under his name.

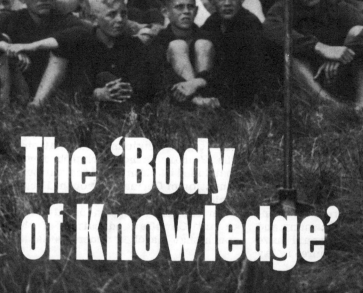

The 'Body of Knowledge'

The vicissitudes of the Weimar Republic also intruded into Germany's educational system, mainly at the level of secondary school and university. While at the beginning it seemed as though the fall of the Hohenzollern Empire had cleared the way for the free run of the reform impulse endeavouring to establish new teacher/student relationships, and to purge the classrooms of their stuffiness, that impulse was soon stifled by the assertion of social, political and religious denominational interest groups. The party struggle on the public forum invaded the classrooms and the lecture halls. If, as in the case of Bernhard Rust, later Hitler's Minister of Science and Education, a teacher actively engaged himself in politics he could expect dismissal, and that with certainty if he was a National Socialist or a Communist. Pupils who, because of their very nature were much more active in their engagement could be prevented from taking the matriculation examination. When, in February 1933, Rust was appointed as 'Prussian Minister of Science and Education' (before the 'coordination' and subjugation of the individual German provinces to the central government in Berlin) one of the first decrees he issued nullified 'all disciplinary measures taken since 1st January 1925 against pupils for actions which had a solely national motivation. Pupils who have been dismissed must be readmitted without previous examination into the forms in which they worked at the time of their dismissal.' Naturally those concerned had themselves celebrated as martyrs for 'the national cause' and made the most of it.

The reluctance to display direct outward political committal by many of the teaching profession was carried

Bernhard Rust addressing a group of youths in Mecklenburg. In 1933 Rust was appointed Hitler's Minister of Science and Education

well into the Third Reich. In 1933 no one could foresee how long Hitler would last, and a substantial body of opinion gave him no longer than any of the previous governments. However, this attitude changed rapidly after the *Reichstag* fire, the March elections and the passing of the Enabling Act. Teachers and Civil Servants alike rushed to become members of the NSDAP or any one of its sub-organisations.

But before that happened, the Hitler Youth in many German urban centres carried out what it considered to be its own seizure of power. From many schools, against the opposition, frequently physical, of headmasters and caretakers, the black, red and gold banner of the republic was torn down from the flagpoles and in its place was flown the banner of Hitler's party. Pictures of prominent Weimar politicians which adorned the walls of class rooms, like that of President Ebert were ceremonially burned in school playgrounds.

After the coordination of the German provinces which thereby extended Rust's responsibility over the whole of Germany he carried out a systematic purge of the entire teaching profession. Teachers at school and university level who had belonged to any one of the 'democratic' parties were removed, mostly by 'premature retirement', a measure which also affected all Jewish teachers irrespective of previous party political affiliation. Men and women who in many cases were better National Socialists than they were teachers replaced them.

The dichotomy between pupils and teachers is probably as old as the relationship between them, and the attitude of 'we' against 'them' was inevitably aggravated by sharp ideological cleavages. But now 'the moment of the youth' had come and many Hitler Youths thought the time ripe to get their own back on the 'liberal bourgeois hypocrites'. One *Jungzugführer* took his unit, broke into his school and in traditional 'beer-hall-battle' manner disrupted and finally dispersed the meeting of a teachers' association. In another case, the windows of the flat of a Latin mistress with a reputation for giving low marks were all smashed by uniformed Hitler Youths who, after they had completed their work, assembled in front of the house and sang sentimental folk songs. When the police arrived they were bewildered. They arrested none of the Hitler Youths but merely took down their names. (The wearing of Hitler Youth uniform carried its advantage throughout Hitler's twelve years. While in uniform no Hitler Youth could be given corporal punishment, which would have been an offence against 'the cloth of honour'. It thus became a very regular practice to wear uniform when a 'storm' was expected to break loose; it was more effective than newspapers stuffed down the backs of trousers.)

Between 1933 and 1934 reports ranging from disobedience to the use of physical force by Hitler Youths against teachers reached such dimensions that the NSDAP too became worried. During the middle of November 1933 the 'National Socialist Committee for Education' met to discuss the threat to school discipline posed by the Hitler Youth and how to meet it. The committee concluded that this was primarily the result of a 'leadership crisis' within the Hitler Youth and that one way of partially meeting it would be to press as many young teachers as possible into service with the Hitler Youth. Obviously the pre-1933 NSDAP members did not aim at a confrontation with the Hitler Youth, but for those who were teachers, Hitler's appointment as Chancellor meant the return to 'law and order'. Rust's ministry declared that 'the authority of the school in the *völkish* state must not be violated' and later, 'It is the task of headmasters to ensure that pupils obey their teachers unconditionally and that law and

order reign supreme throughout the schools'. Some ideas on the function of the school were expressed in the sentence 'The supreme task of the schools is the education of youth for the service of Volk and State in the National Socialist spirit. Any controlling function is to be exercised solely by the immediately superior administrative organ'. This last sentence was added by the NSDAP itself lest Hitler Youths interpreted their role as being one of controlling the teachers. From the point of view of Nazi teachers then, the Hitler Youth's function was supplementary to that of the school, not superior. And in order to reassure schools as well as parents the Hitler Youth was explicity admonished that 'it had to respect the authority of the school unconditionally, and its leaders are to remind their members fully to fulfill the demands of the school. School as well as Hitler Youth in their demands upon the youth have to respect the participation of the parents as well as the maintenance of

Teenagers at the Festival of German Schools in the Berlin stadium, 1933

a healthy family life. In the new state the family in particular represents the germinal seed and basis of the *Volkstüm*, its existence is to be furthered and protected.' While other youth organisations which continued to exist until 1936 were not allowed to wear uniform at school the Hitler Youth was. Rust also introduced the German salute *Heil Hitler* which each master had to give when entering the class room, the pupils replying in the same manner. When pupil or pupils met masters in the corridor they saluted one another silently just by raising the right arm. The inevitable result of the compulsory introduction of the party salute was a growing sloppiness in its execution and the formula of *Heil Hitler* just being cut down to a simple *Heil* or during the war *Heil und Sieg* (Hail and Victory). 'Non-Aryans' had the choice of saluting or not, an option which had

99

become fictional with the growing wave of Jewish emigration and the removal of Jewish pupils into specially set up Jewish schools.

After 1936 when the *Reichsjugend-führung* had become an official state institution it began once again to assert its right to participate in the decision-making process concerning school policy. It expected greater toleration by the schools for Hitler Youth activities which interferred with the school curriculum such as granting of special leave for Hitler Youth leaders sent on special 'leadership' courses. Furthermore, teachers were instructed to exercise great tact in dealing with Hitler Youth leaders in their forms in order not to damage their prestige in the eyes of their comrades and subordinates.'

Nevertheless, after 1936 when the Hitler Youth had been nationally institutionalized relations between the Hitler Youth and the schools improved, time schedules were more coordinated to meet each others needs than had been the case between 1933 and 1936.

Any look at the organisational structure of the Hitler Youth will show that its affairs overlapped with many of the old as well as newly established ministries. The Ministry of the Interior, the Ministry of 'Propaganda and Popular Enlightenment', the labour service and the army as well as the SS were all concerned to some extent with youth affairs. The army and the party had of course different ideas as to what the desirable product of National Socialist education should be. These 'educational principles' found expression in Hitler Youth leadership training which con-

sisted of three week courses each totalling 170 hours. Of these 105 hours were spent on 'physical training', divided up into 49 hours cross-country sports, 40 hours physical exercises and 16 hours rifle shooting. A total of 65 hours was spent on 'ideological training', comprising 37 hours political instruction, 3 hours of political seminars and the remainder on some of the more practical aspects of Hitler Youth leadership such as how to run small group meetings and discussions.

In 1935, the year in which Hitler renounced disarmament clauses of the Versailles treaty, was for the Hitler Youth the *Jahr der Ertüchtigung* (Year of Training) serving a dual purpose – that of getting a maximum intake of recruits already prepared through paramilitary training for 1936 and also to excite the active interest of the youth in the forthcoming 1936 Olympic Games. Early in March 1935 the first Reichs skiing competitions of the Hitler Youth took place, while in July of the same year motorised competitions were held, preceded by the German Youth Festival at the end of June 1935 in which nearly 3,500 Hitler Youths participated.

Inevitably, paramilitary training was given priority over that of simple sports. But this raised the question as to who should provide and supervise the training, a question which immediately brought the army into the picture since it alone had the necessary resources. The SS-*Verfügungstruppen* at the time could hardly be considered since they themselves were in the process of rigorous training partially carried out by army officers delegated for the task. The army, of course, saw in the Hitler Youth as well as in the younger age groups of the storm troopers an ideal reservoir of manpower well suited for the plans envisaging the rapid expansion of Germany's armed forces. At purely local levels, cooperation between army officers and Hitler Youth units already existed, but the attempt to institutionalize this re-

Even for the girls paramilitary training was given priority over simple sports. Here 2,500 Berlin schoolgirls rehearse for the Olympic mass physical training demonstration

lationship was not made before 1937 when the then Lieutenant-Colonel Erwin Rommel, at the time an instructor at the War Academy in Potsdam, was assigned to the Hitler Youth to supervise their general standards of training and discipline. A wearer of Germany's highest decoration of the First World War, the *Pour le Merite* he was an immediate subject of hero-worship by the boys. The same cannot be said about Rommel's relations with *Reichsjugendführer* Baldur von Schirach. By comparison with the battle-hardened soldier, Schirach, in his attempts to assert himself, was bound to appear bombastic and effete. Rommel had nothing against the paramilitary training of the Hitler Youth, but the acquisition of a sound educational grounding coupled with good

character building were more important to him. He despised the kind of upper echelon Hitler Youth leader in a chauffeur driven car. As the son of a schoolmaster, Rommel could very well appreciate the difficulties between Hitler Youth and educational authorities and on a number of occasions sided with the latter against the former. When Rommel tried to act as a mediator between Rust's Ministry and Schirach, the Hitler Youth leader took offence. Rommel told him point blank that if he was determined to be the leader of a paramilitary force he should first become a soldier himself. It was the end of Rommel's assignment with the Hitler Youth and thus the ending of any formal relationship between army and Hitler Youth.

Hitler obviously had a different conception of the education of German youth from that held by the German army. Between the two extremes there existed variants, but all of them were characterised by a torrent of ague phraseology rather than by a clearly defined educational concept. One Nazi educationalist stated that the aim of education was the creation of a 'political soldier', another that it ought to produce an 'ethos of service' and yet another exclaimed that the objective of educational policy should be the inculcation of 'Faith, obedience and fighting'.

One member of the legal department of the *Reichsjugendführung* contrasted the objective of a humanities-oriented education which for him culminated in the concept of 'love' with the new National Socialist ideals of 'lack of compromise, preparedness to fight, enthusiasm for the cause and deep faith in National Socialist ideology', reduced by him to the common denominator of 'honour'. The concept of 'love', he suggested, was responsible for an excess of compassion, subjection and humility, but the concept of 'honour' would produce a race of unconquerable fighters. While love kills personality because of its 'internationalism', the concept of 'honour' as it would be indoctrinated into the minds of German youth would produce the perfect national community, the perfect racial *Volk*. The existing schools were to purvey the traditional empirical body of knowledge, but ultimately it would be the NSDAP in the form of the Hitler Youth which would mould every child of a German mother and father into a 'true German'. Within the educational system of the Third Reich the Hitler Youth was to occupy the same position with regard to Germany's youth as the Nazi party occupied with regard to adult Germans. The ultimate objective was that every teacher would be the product of the National Socialist system of education and thus resolve the dichotomy between school and Hitler Youth.

Hitler frequently expressed his own low opinion of the teaching profession, which he believed should ideally comprise women only. No doubt his resentment was based on the experi-

ence of his own schooldays in Austria and in *Mein Kampf* he names only one exception, his pan-German history teacher, the man he was to meet again during the *Anschluss* at Linz. In spite of Hitler's low estimation of the profession a considerable number of the pre-1923 old guard had been teachers, the most notorious among them Julius Streicher, and in 1929 a 'National Socialist Teachers' League' was founded which issued the regular monthly *The German Educator*, and after 1933 all teachers, unless they wished to change their positions or to retire prematurely, were compelled to join it. But once they had joined they began to be so overburdened with additional duties as Hitler Youth Leaders or in other party functions that their quality as teachers seriously deteriorated and with it the educational level of their pupils. In 1943 a member of the *Reichsjugendführung* compiled a report about the general situation of the educational sector in Germany. The author of the report was extremely outspoken and that in itself was an exception at a time when every subordinate was only too eager to draw the most favourable picture for his superiors. The report stated that after the war, the consequences of the war apart, of every hundred grammar school teachers required only thirty-five would be available. While during the inter-war years thirty per cent of all university candidates intended to study philology, in a faculty which comprised a range of subjects essential for the majority of grammar school teachers, the percentage had sunk to ten per cent in 1939 and to five per cent in 1941. The decline in the prestige of the intellectual professions and the growing attraction of competing occupations accounted in the main for this shortage.

While the Weimar Republic had made attempts to raise the level of primary school teachers, after 1933 it became regular practice to take into consideration work done actively for the NSDAP thereby relieving applicants of the need for professional examinations which had previously been compulsory. Institutionalized shortcuts such as 'Institutes for Teacher Training' ran short cramming courses and its members wore Hitler Youth uniforms throughout and were organised along Hitler Youth lines. The outbreak of war produced an acute shortage of teachers and this provided the opportunity for the Hitler Youth to participate directly in remodelling teacher training courses in order to produce the 'political teacher'. Hitler Youth leaders and headmasters were directed to observe their subordinates and pupils respectively for two qualities: 'leadership quality' and 'teaching ability'. Those endowed with the first quality would be asked to go through special examinations which, if passed, would get them a scholarship at one of the 'élite' schools; those who displayed an ability to teach would be encouraged to take up the teaching profession. Selection for teache training was made jointly by official of the Ministry of Education an representativs of the Hitler Youth The heads of the training institute were to be, in principle, Hitler Yout leaders though in fact the incessan demand for manpower during the wa did not allow the full implementatio of this system. Teachers were als to be recruited among Hitler Yout leaders with the ultimate objectiv of creating a teaching body 'unite and strengthened by membership i one organisation, an instrument clos to the political leadership whic would disseminate a political shape through every facet of education.

While these 'ideals' were awaitin fulfilment, schools still had to be ru with the existing personnel, th curriculum still contained a good dea with which the 'reformers' would hav dispensed. Before the war the firs schools directly affected by Hitler' rule were the religious denominationa schools which were abolished in 1936 a clear breach of the Concorda Whether this step had detriment effects upon the pupils is a matter opinion. From this time, Catholic and Protestants were educated in th same school, dividing up into thei respective denominations once a wee in order to receive an hour of religiou instruction. During the same yea church holidays during week day were no longer kept as public holiday and special prayers on such occasion were banned at school. Two year later all teachers were ordered t resign from any denomination a organisation.

German language teaching bega to ignore the classics in favour of study of the German heritage and th German united community. Litera ture was chosen to illustrate th bonds unifying the community in thei present struggle. But literature fo this purpose was extremely hard t come by, and only two alternative remained: recourse to war book written by National Socialists o

approved by them, or a return to the classics, excluding those written by Germans of the Jewish faith.

History was also a subject heavily affected and all history text books were subjected to a thorough revision. The first history text book this author received at a grammar school in 1943 began with Adolf Hitler and ended with Hannibal. History was exclusively politico-military, depicting a continuous struggle by the German people for power and existence.

National Socialist education took to the extreme a tendency inherent in German historiography since the nineteenth century – the concentration upon 'the world historical individual'. History could almost be taught in terms of political and military biographies. Recent history which was introduced from the first form at the primary school was exclusively the history of the NSDAP, with a strong mixture of National Socialist hero-worship and mythology. guidelines for the teaching of history in the sixth-form in grammar schools

Faces that would shape the future and for which it was being shaped. The notion of an Ayran elite was fundamental to Hitler's brand of National Socialism

laid down that the period between 1918 and 1932 was to be treated as the attempt by Germany to realise the western European ideas of 1789. Political Catholicism was to be portrayed as an ally of the Marxist and capitalist International. The expansion of Jewish world dominion in Germany was to be demonstrated and parliamentary democracy was to be interpreted as an inevitable step in the process of the seizure of power by the Bolsheviks. Finally January 1933 brought about Germany's liberation through the hands of Adolf Hitler. Geography was to be taught in terms of geopolitics, of living space, of demographic movements, racial expansion and acquisition of colonial territory.

In the natural sciences biology was the subject worst affected through racial teachings. Unverified and absurd theories found their way into the textbooks with the purpose of producing a 'racial sense' and 'racial instinct' in Germany's youth. Even arithmetic problems were designed to influence children ideologically: The question 'How many children must a family produce in order to secure the quantitative continuance of the German Volk?' was not unusual. Children also faced more grisly problems such as, 'A mentally handicapped person costs the public 4 Reichsmark per day, a cripple 5.50 Reichsmark and a convicted criminal 3.50 Reichsmark. Cautious estimates state that within the boundaries of the German Reich 300,000 persons are being cared for in public institutions. How many marriage loans at 1,000 Reichsmark per couple could annually be financed from the funds allocated to institutions?'

However, because the 'political teacher' could not be produced in sufficient quantities in time, education was mainly left in the hands of those who had carried out the task for decades. Many, if not most, were nationalistic, though only a minority were rabid National Socialists. For the most part lip service was paid to Nazi ideals during lessons followed by a quick transition, as in the case of German literature, to the German classics, or the staple fare on which the teachers themselves had been trained in pre-1914 or pre-1933 days.

An important byproduct of this discrepancy between 'theory' and 'practice' in the teaching profession was a sense of insecurity among teachers – fear of the risk of being denounced. Though actual cases of this happening were very rare, a teacher in German literature who for lack of National Socialist material put the emphasis of his teaching upon the masters of the past, was risking a potential challenge by a member of the form he instructed. And this sense of insecurity was further aggravated by the awareness, as in Biology,

that what one was teaching was little more than complete nonsense. Insecurity bred uncertainty, and uncertainty led to a lowering of educational standards. When, as well as this, 'Total War' mobilised most of the German youth in one form or another, when entire school-days were devoted to the collection of scrap metal, when entire grammar school forms manned aircraft batteries and teachers taught them in between raids, education as such hardly existed at all.

What applied to primary and secondary education applied equally to university education. Universities, probably more than any other educational institution in Germany, were strongholds of National Socialism, even before 1933. Schirach's NS-Students' League aimed at creating a new type of student, a new type of university teacher and a new concept of 'the body of knowledge'. Coordination of the universities started in May 1933 and from the point of view of unifying a spiritually divided nation it was probably not a bad thing to abolish exclusive student corporations and to prohibit the barbaric habit of duelling. But in place of student corporations stepped the all-inclusive NS-Students' League and no one would be admitted to a university or allowed to continue studying at one unless he was a member. As a branch of the *Reichsjugendführung* of the Hitler Youth, students who were not already members of the Hitler Youth had within their organisation to carry out much the same duties as the schoolboy Hitler Youth. 'Physical exercise' and para-military training supervised by the army became compulsory. The new type of student was to be very much the same thing as 'the new type of German youth' which the Hitler Youth set out to produce. As in the schools, so at the universities the teaching body's complaints increased about the excessive extra-mural activities of the students which diverted them from their scholarly pursuits and led to a general lowering of

Physical training – a prerequisite of self-improvement. Teachers at the universities soon complained that the importance attached to sport left too little time for scholarly pursuits

standards.

The creation of a new type of university teacher proved as difficult as in the lower sectors of education. The 'political teacher' in this sphere proved an unattained objective, with some exceptions of course. What was achieved was of a purely negative nature, the exclusion and expulsion of German university teachers of the Jewish faith, or of Socialist inclination. Between November 1932 and July 1933 the number of German university teachers had decreased by 7.5 per cent. By the end of 1935 a total of 1,684 German university teachers had been dismissed, the majority of them (about sixty-two per cent) Germans of the Jewish faith. The road to the 'political teacher' was paved with dismissals of some of Germany's most fertile scientific brains.

As far as a new formulation of 'the body of knowledge' was concerned, this remained as nebulous in the field of higher education as in the field of secondary education and in fact never bridged the stultifying wall of meaningless political hyperbole.

Training the elite

To create an elite within the Hitler Youth two institutions were founded, the *Nationalpolitischen Erziehungsanstalten* (NPEA or NAPOLA) and the *Adolf Hitler Schulen*. While the NAPOLA was designed to produce an élite which could fill posts in all spheres of German life, political, administrative, economic, military as well as academic, the *Adolf Hitler* schools were geared explicity to produce party leaders. These schools, the first of which were established in January 1937, were defined as units of the Hitler Youth and supervised by the NSDAP and the *Reichsjugendführung*. The AHS comprised essentially six forms and a pupil would enter at the age of twelve, after having distinguished himself at school and in the service of the *Jungvolk* and upon the recommendation of his immediate superiors and the local party leaders. Education at an AHS was state-financed and meant to lead to matriculation standard although its pupils were not expected to go to university but instead to attend a special party leadership school. The immediate superior of each AHS was the local *Gauleiter*. There were no traditional style formal examinations or school reports but each year a so-called 'effort competition' took place, in which pupils competed for places in the form above them. At the age of eighteen a pupil was to be awarded a special diploma by Hitler personally and then to do his labour and military service. Upon completion of this (at which time he was expected to have married), he was to be called to a three and a half year course at a party academy, an *Ordensburg* (the castle of the order) and then move into a leading position in the party. The very best pupils were to attend a course at the *Hochschule der NSDAP*

A still photograph from a Nazi film about the NAPOLA, an institution designed to produce an elite which would then fill the leading positions in all strata of national life

A *Jungvolk* leader holds a fingernail inspection before a meal at an AHS

(the higher institute of party) which would school them for party leadership at a high level. This institute, to be headed by Alfred Rosenberg, was in fact never built; the war put an end to the project. A total of nine AHSs were founded in 1938 and the first 'graduates' emerged in 1942 after a shortened course.

In contrast to the AHS, which was an institution without precedent, the antecedents of the NAPOLA went back via the Weimar Republic to the cadet institutes for the training of future officers of Imperial Germany and of Prussia, first founded early in the 18th Century by Frederick William I who emulated the example set by Louis XIV. Officially the *Kadettenanstalten* were dissolved on Allied orders in 1920, but some of them continued during the Weimar Republic as *State Institutes of Education* or as private 'public schools' in which a

special emphasis was placed on 'soldierly traditions'. Hitler's forty-fourth birthday in 1933 provided the occasion for the foundation of the first three NAPOLAs; five more followed in 1934 and seven in 1935 of which the majority had previously been cadet institutes. Nine more followed in 1941 and between 1942 and 1944 a total of eighteen were founded of which two were for female pupils. NAPOLAs were also founded outside Germany where they were termed *Reichsschulen*, two of these were started in Holland at Valkenberg near Maastricht and Heijthuijsen and one in Belgium at Quatrecht near Ghent.

While the basis of the AHS was that of a 'party school', the NAPOLA was to produce the 'political soldier' who could be used on all 'fronts', that is to say in all spheres of German public activity. Unlike the AHS, the

Training on how to use a rifle – part of the curriculum at the Adolf Hitler Schools

NAPOLA was not directly a party institution and therefore not subordinate to the NSDAP. Its immediate superior authority was the Ministry of Science and Education, its curriculum essentially that of a grammar school; some of the NAPOLAs catered for the humanities and others for the natural sciences and modern languages. Neither the position of *Gauleiter* nor any other party office had any supervisory function, and the Hitler Youth gained influence only in so far as from 1936 onwards all NAPOLA pupils had to be members of the *Jungvolk* or the HJ. The organisation within each school was modelled closely on that of the army; there were no forms but 'platoons' and 'companies' and each company carried the tradition of one historically famous German regiment. But while

NAPOLA entrants learning to march. The aim of these institutions was to produce a generation of 'political soldiers'

A grandiose setting for the dissemination of grandiose ideas – the first NAPOLA at Lissa

in the old cadet institutes the teachers had mostly been army officers, this function in the NAPOLA was fulfilled by civilians who shared living accommodation with their pupils. An attempt to emulate the British public school system can be discerned, but unlike the public schools the NAPOLA lacked the class basis; its pupils came from all social levels throughout Germany and in cases where the payment of school fees was not possible it was usually waived.

The actual founder of the NAPOLA, Joachim Haupt, came from the German Youth movement and endeavoured to carry its traditions into the schools. August Heissmeyer, the second inspector of the NAPOLA, came from the Youth movement and during the early years of the recruitment of teachers those with a youth movement background had a clear

advantage over those whose youth activities had been confined solely to the party-political sphere.

When the NAPOLAs were first founded their principals were allowed considerable liberty in the choosing of their staff and the criteria of selection were academic rather than political. Although Hitler's preference for physical rather than intellectual education could not be completely ignored, the aim was nevertheless to fuse the traditions of the cadet corps of the German army with those of the British public school, or rather with what British public school traditions were taken to be. National Socialist educationalists understood the British public school system in so far as it rested on a clearly defined community basis. They compared their own system of élitist education with the British system in the following terms: 'The boy at an early age is removed from the spoiling influence of the parental home, and at first has difficulty in establishing his own position. But simply the need to survive as a rule wakens the necessary forces in him, which give him hardness and security and a firmness of will.

'By means of the strictly authoritarian prefect and fagging system he gets accustomed to obey as well as to give orders and by stages he acquires new rights within a system of an authoritarian self-administration . . . Public schools are therefore explicit instruments for shaping the individual pupil into a uniform national type with an equally uniform system of values.

'Our most recent educational endeavours in the National Political Educational Institutes . . . appear to be run along the same principles. Like the public schools in England they are meant to train an élite, a reservoir for leadership. The principle of a common education within an institution is also pursued essentially by compulsory participation of all in sports, and in general by physical and intellectual training within a small com-

munity. Team competition is more highly valued than individual achievement. By stressing a healthy way of life damages created earlier on by overfeeding pupils with dry knowledge will be eradicated. That does not mean that they [the NAPOLAs] do not convey regular and thorough instruction. Through strengthening historical consciousness, German consciousness . . . awakening the thought of the national community wider political perspectives are being created which ultimately culminate in an organic view of the whole . . . Teachers and pupils are themselves a product of careful selection, what is decisive is the character. The aim of the education is to produce a *Führer* – a leader educated to think in terms of the community as a whole. As in public schools, the authoritarian principle is indispensable . . . [and] the tutorial system also has its German equivalent.'

On the one hand emphasis was placed upon duty, courage and sim-

plicity, and on the other the attributes of the 'colonial ruler', an air of superiority, impeccable manners and style, while at the same time absolute dedication to the National Socialist 'ideology' was nurtured. The three together would make up a new class of leaders, drawn not from one social class but from all social classes within Germany.

The NAPOLA tried to combine the triple functions carried out by school, Hitler Youth and home and a high level of academic performance was expected from all its pupils.

As already indicated NAPOLAs were subject to inspection by the Ministry of Science and Education. Promotions within the teaching body of NAPOLAS went through the department of the Ministry responsible for all personnel promotions. Nominally, the teaching appointments were made by Hitler himself, but that was a mere formality, teachers had to possess all the qualifications normally necessary at a German grammar school.

Regimented walking party. Team competition was more highly stressed than individual achievement

Joachim Haupt, who had been a tutor of the Ploen State Institute of Education during the Weimar Republic, stressed the significance of his choice of the name for these schools. 'National political' should imply the strong ties of the school with the state rather than with the party which, for instance, the title 'National Socialist' would have suggested. Moreover, by establishing an identity distinct from the party he hoped to drive home the message that youth had to be led by youth, a message which, however, he qualified by pointing out that any political education that would benefit the state would necessarily be carried out by adults only. Schirach immediately suspected a potential rival in Haupt and the June purge of 1934 provided the necessary pretext for his replacement. Fortunately for Haupt, he did not share the fate of Röhm and others. Originally it was planned that each teacher or tutor besides being a civil servant should also have a rank corresponding with his position in the SA. After June 1934 this idea was dropped to be taken up again by Haupt's successor, August Heissmeyer, with the proviso that instead of SA commissions teachers were to hold commissions of the SS.

Schirach was not the only one who wished to exercise some influence in the NAPOLAs. The uniforms worn by the pupils were evidence of the influences exercised by the army and the navy. Late in the war, but by no means at all NAPOLAs, the uniforms issued were similar to those of *Waffen-SS*, the field grey a minute shade darker than the field grey of the army, the eagle on the left sleeve of the jacket instead of on the collar. To be caught by the Allies wearing this uniform meant some months as a prisoner of war – even for eleven and twelve year-olds.

The process of the selection of the pupils for the NAPOLA was laid down personally by Rust and formalised in a ministerial directive in October 1937 in which Rust stated 'It is of utmost importance that the *Nationalpolitische Erziehungsanstalten* receive those German boys who, in their attitude and ability, meet the special requirements of these institutes. I therefore order:

1) Every elementary school pupil of the third or fourth form who seems suitable for a NAPOLA should be mentioned to the local school administration by 1st November of each year. Its head will then forward the proposals to the nearest NAPOLA via the official channels. A list of them is enclosed.

2) Heads of NAPOLAs or individuals delegated by them, as well as representatives of the local administration, shall be enabled to attend the lessons of primary school forms of which candidates are members as well as attend the examinations leading to

admission to grammar schools.'

Naturally every selection was determined on 'racial' grounds, nor could physically handicapped candidates be admitted. These were the only obstacles for an applicant. Wealth and social status were irrelevant. Provisions were also made to allow the entrance of 'late developers'. In their selection process the NAPOLAs could afford a high measure of selectivity. Only those whose appearance as well as their scholarship measured up to their high standards were allowed in.

Pre-selections were carried out between October and December of each year, conducted by the doctor of the NAPOLA and several teachers in the localities of the candidates. On an average each NAPOLA received annually 400 applications, of which only approximately 100 were allowed to take the entrance examination. About one third of those passed the examination.

The decision to put forward an elementary school pupil for entry was entirely out of the hands of his parents. In the case of the author, the proposal was put forward by the head of the school who also happened to be the local party leader. My mother, a widow, with one son already at the front in Russia, went to see the head of the school, insisting that as a widow and with one son already in the armed forces she should not be forced to part with her youngest. The headmaster's reply was 'My dear lady, you had better adjust your ideas. Your son is not your personal property, solely at your disposal. He is on loan to you but he is the property of the German *Volk*. To object to his name being put forward for an élite school is tantamount to insulting the Führer and Reich.' My mother's protest was in vain.

The examination took place at one of the NAPOLAs and lasted a week. There were variations from school to school but basically it amounted to four hours of general subjects in the morning, comprising German compo-

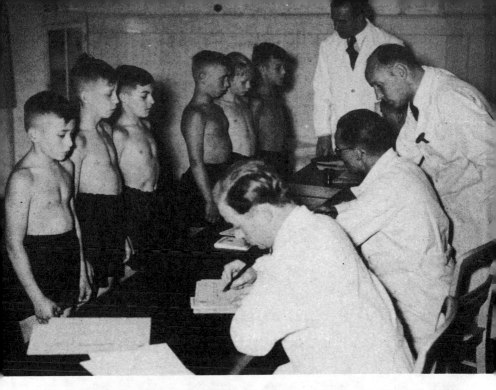

Candidates for the NAPOLA line up for a medical examination – part of the pre-selection process carried out each year. Of some 400 applicants, only 100 were allowed to sit the entrance examination

sition, spelling, arithmetic and vivas in the pupil's main subjects as well as tests in history, geography, biology and general knowledge. The afternoons were taken up with physical exercises, like swimming (or a 'courage test' for those who could not swim who were thrown into the deep end of the swimming pool), athletics, obstacle races and a field exercise which included map reading. Exercises also took place during the night. They often took the form of a para-military exercise – the capture of a forest bridge occupied by another team, or being dropped from the sidecar of a motorcycle miles from anywhere and ordered to make one's way back before dawn.

The selection procedure was meant to ensure the inclusion of the talent of all social strata. Statistics again are very fragmentary, but records in existence at Oranienstein produce the following breakdown of the social origins for the 1938 intake in that region:—

Of a total of eighty-two boys 9 were sons of workers, 7 were commercial employees (non-executive), 20 were civil servants, 5 were teachers, 20 were self employed, 8 were army officers and party (SA) leaders, 6 were artisans, 3 were farmers, 4 were doctors.

Preferential treatment was often given by the selection committees to the sons of the 'old fighters' and those whose fathers had either been killed in the war or had suffered heavy physical injuries in the course of it. The Oranienstein example seems to suggest that in practice neither category benefited very much. In the 1943 intake at Bensberg near Cologne there was not a single pupil whose father was an NSDAP member, but the

NAPOLA students on a military exercise

Learning the art of field communications

Social origins of the Hitler Youth

Father's occupation ▼	Intake sample of 82 boys at Oranienstein, 1938
Civil servants	20
Self employed	20
Manual workers	9
Army officers and party (SA) leaders	8
Commercial employees (non executive)	7
Artisans	6
Teachers	5
Doctors	4
Farmers	3

Above: The Adolf Hitler Youth Hostel at Berchtesgaden. Below: Hitler reviews his 'future troops' at an Adolf Hitler school at Obersalzburg

majority had served at the front.

School fees were determined by the income of the parents and ranged from 20 *Reichsmark* to 150 *Reichsmark* per month (according to the official conversion of those days, from £1 to £7.10.0d.). During the first six years of the NAPOLA's existence free places or scholarships were rare; after the outbreak of war, however, they increased rapidly and taking again the 1943 Bensberg example, only three NAPOLA pupils paid any fees at all. The position was similar with textbooks, exercise-books and so on. At first parents had to pay for them in full or in part but later they were issued free.

The German military successes up to the autumn of 1942, and with them the feasibility of the creation of a 'Germanic Empire', had their effects also on the educational concepts held by the leaders of the Third Reich and especially those concerning the training of the future élite. On 10th December 1940 Hitler gave a great speech before a mass gathering of armaments workers in Berlin in which he referred to the élite schools 'You all know,' he said, 'we have the National Political Education Institutes and the Adolf Hitler Schools. Into these schools we bring the gifted children of the masses, sons of workers, of peasants, whose parents would normally never be in a position to pay for the higher education of their children . . . Thus we have created great opportunities to build up this state from below. This is our aim. It is a marvellous thing to be able to fight for an ideal like this. It is marvellous that we can say that our aim lies almost within the realm of fantasy, that we imagine a state in which in future every position will be occupied by the ablest sons of our people, irrespective of their origin, a state in which birth means nothing and achievement and ability everything . . . But this image is confronted by a different one, that of another world. There, the ultimate aim remains the accumulation of wealth, of capital, the struggle for family property, the struggle caused by the egotism of the individual. Everything else is simply a means to an end. These two worlds are the ones that confront each other today.

'We know quite well that if we lose this struggle this would not merely be the end of our socialist work of construction, but the end of the German people as a whole. The other world, however, says, "If we lose, then the entire capitalist structure will collapse. We have hoarded gold and put it into our cellars. It would lose its entire value. Because if the idea spreads among the peoples that work is the decisive factor what then? Then we will have bought our gold for nothing . . ." They can all see quite clearly how our nation is being restructured: on their side we see a state governed by a thin crust, the upper class who send their sons automatically to their specific educational institutions like Eton College. On our side we see the Adolf Hitler Schools and the National Political Educational Institutes. Two worlds. In the one case the children of the people, in the other, only the sons of a financial aristocracy. These are two worlds. I admit one of the two worlds will have to break, either one or the other . . .'

The speech was the signal for the mushroom growth of new NAPOLAs which, between 1941 and 1944, took place predominantly in Germany's frontier provinces. Military success encouraged visions of the 'master race'. In place of the idea of securing living space for the German people and concentrating all Germans in the heart of Europe, now stepped the idea of an empire, resting upon the shoulders of the Germanic race.

On 5th April 1942 at Hitler's headquarters, during dinner, Himmler declared that, in his view, the best way of settling the French problem would be to carry off every year a certain number of racially healthy children,

Heinrich Himmler. His obsession with
the superiority of the Germanic 'race'
led him to pronounce a solution to the
'French problem'

chosen among France's Germanic
population. It would be necessary to
try to settle these children, while still
very young, in German boarding
schools, to train them away from their
French nationality, which was due to
chance, to make them aware of their
Germanic blood and thus inculcate
into them the notion of their membership of the great group of Germanic
peoples. Hitler did not promise himself much success of this policy, 'The
mass of the French people,' he declared, 'has "petty Bourgeois"
spiritual inclinations, so much so that
it would be a triumph to succeed in
removing the elements of Germanic
origin from the grasp of the country's
ruling class.' The *Reichsführer* SS
then spoke of the creation in Holland
of two *Nationalpolitischer Erziehungsanstalten* for boys and one for girls to
be called 'Reichs schools' – a title
approved by the Führer. A third of the
pupils would be Dutch and two-thirds
German. After a certain period, the
Dutch pupils would have to visit a
German NAPOLA. The Reichsführer
SS explained that, to guarantee that
instruction would be given in accor-

dance with the purposes of the
Germanic Reich he refused to claim a
financial contribution from Holland
and had asked Schwarz (the Reichs
Treasurer) to set aside a specific sum
exclusively for the financing of these
schools. A project was also being
considered for the creation of similar
schools in Norway, They, too, would
be financed solely by the Reichs
Treasurer. 'If we want to prevent
Germanic blood from penetrating into
the ruling class of the peoples whom
we dominate, and subsequently turning against us, we shall have gradually
to subject all the precious Germanic
elements to the influence of this
instruction.' The Führer approved of
this point of view. 'Under no circumstances should one make the mistake
of training apparently racially valuable members of other nations in the
German Wehrmacht before having
ensured the ideological orientation
upon the Germanic Reich . . .'

Similar procedures of racial selection and training at NAPOLAs were
to be applied in all other German-
occupied territories. However, besides
the Dutch and Belgian NAPOLAS,
only the NAPOLA at Rufach in Alsace
had a substantial proportion of non-
Germans, the majority were racial
Germans from the South Tyrol,
Bessarabia and Bukovina. One basic
principle was insisted upon, namely,
that whoever gained access to a
NAPOLA, whether German or non-
German, whether West of East European, was to have equal opportunities
for advancement. Whether in practice
this principle would have ever been
followed is a question that was never
put to the test.

It is doubtful whether, without
Himmler's direct influence, so many
NAPOLAs would have been set up
from 1941 onwards. The Adolf-Hitler
Schools were a creation outside the
sphere of the Ministry of Science and
Education, but the NAPOLAs re-
mained an integral part of Germany's
national system of education.
Himmler established his influence in

Above: 'Germany is where our hearts are'. Brave admission of non-German pupils to one of the Reich schools founded by Himmler. *Below:* Training in marksmanship at a Hitler Youth summer camp

the NAPOLAs slowly but steadily and subtly. At first he simply appeared as an honorary guest at their foundations, but later declared the readiness of the SS to finance the cost of the uniforms and the equipment. With the appointment of Heissmeyer as Inspector of the NAPOLAs, the first SS-*Gruppenführer* of the general SS made his appearance in the system. This provided Himmler with an advantage over the army by which he hoped to gain a more direct and explicit influence upon the NAPOLAs. The army intended to have officers and NCOs made instructors but upon Himmler's instructions Heissmeyer refused to allow this. In their place Waffen-SS officers were temporarily delegated to NAPOLAs to supervise paramilitary training. From 1941 onwards the SS also supervised the 'racial' aspect of the selection process. However, Heissmeyer, although an SS officer and a convinced National Socialist, had his own ideas about how the NAPOLAs should be run and the kind of teachers they should have. The relatively large amount of independence which he allowed the heads of the schools and the teachers he felt could only be maintained as long as they remained under Rust's Ministry and did not become an exclusive domain for the SS. This brought him into conflict with both Himmler and *SS-Gruppenführer* Berger, the protagonist of the 'Germanic SS'. The final result was that the *Reichsschulen* outside Germany came directly under the control of the *SS-Hauptamt*, the remainder was left with Heissmeyer who was instructed to do his utmost to see that his graduates would volunteer for the *Waffen*-SS. This did not eliminate the existing friction because the independence the heads of the NAPOLAs enjoyed allowed them to turn down 'undesirable' lecturers, such as those provided by the SS. Heissmeyer fell between two stools. Rust suspected him of intrigue on behalf of Himmler, Himmler accused him of not furthering the interest of

the SS sufficiently. As in the course of the war the internal balance of power tilted in favour of the SS its ultimate supremacy was assured and from 1942 onwards a great number of experienced NAPOLA teachers were drafted into the armed forces and replaced by SS-nominees. Inevitably, Rust was losing his position and this was confirmed when, in December 1944, Hitler issued a special *Führerbefehl* appointing Himmler personally as supervisor of all schools from which, in future, officers for the Wehrmacht and the Waffen-SS were to be recruited.

The curriculum within the various NAPOLAs varied considerably but for the upper forms it consisted of four hours of German weekly, three hours of history, two hours of geography, four hours of Latin, five hours of English, three hours of mathematics, two hours of art, one hour of religious instruction, one hour of music, and five hours of sport. But in contrast to the curriculum of traditional German grammar schools which taught academic subjects in the morning and left the afternoon for sports, NAPOLAs began at eight o'clock in the morning with two hours of lessons followed by three hours of sports which could mean cross country exercises, riding, sailing or, for the older ones, driving lessons. Afternoons would follow a similar pattern, beginning with academic subjects and then moving on either to arts, music or athletics. The impression to be conveyed to the pupils was that education was not simply a process of book learning but the interaction of intellectual, physical, artistic and political faculties. Relationships inside the school took their model from the military code and political activities were carried out within the ranks of the Jungvolk or the HJ. Already, from the first year onwards, NAPOLA pupils were compelled to involve themselves with the activities of the surrounding community. While the younger ones would work with farmers gathering the harvests, and digging potatoes or picking fruit, the older ones were sent to work in the steel foundries or in the coal mines. The report on each individual's performance in these capacities was as important in his final assessment as a pupil as were his academic or other achievements.

One vital element in furthering 'the spirit of the community' was frequent community celebrations, either of national holidays which were celebrated with considerable pomp, or of the awards to pupils. The mysterious magnetism of the roaring log fires in the NAPOLA yard exercised upon the individual pupil the same fascination as the camp fires of old and gave him the sense of 'belonging', *Du bist nichts, Dein Volk ist alles* – 'You are nothing, your people is everything'.

Before the war one of the main

A gardening class. Young children were encouraged from the start to involve themselves with all the activities of the community

A group of young students head for the fields. Fruit picking and hay making were comparably enjoyable tasks; older students were often sent to work in the steel foundries or in the coal mines

features of the final year was an exchange visit to a school abroad. Visits of this kind were usually arranged on an exchange basis. Pupils of St Paul's, London, visited Oranienstein, while its own pupils went to London. The German reports about Britain make interesting reading. They stress the importance of tradition on the one hand, a lack of toughness in games on the other. What seemed to astonish them most was how 'ill-informed' the English were on the subject of Hitler's Germany and the extent to which they believed the 'anti-German propaganda'. Pupils from Harrow also visited Oranienstein in 1936; an Anglo-German football matched ended in a draw while the British won the fencing

competition. Among other schools included in NAPOLA-sponsored Anglo-German visits was Dauntsey's School in West Lavington. But the reports submitted were all fairly uniform. Friendly reception, the impact of the historical consciousness of the average Briton, general helpfulness but strong hostility on a purely political level. The British press is generally described by the visitors as 'anti-German' with the notable exception of the *Times*.

Exchange visits continued up to and including 1938. They were also arranged between teachers. One British teacher described his experiences thus:— 'I spent the whole of last year in one of these NAPOLAs, and visited a large number of other boarding schools in Germany; and I propose now briefly to describe the kind of life the boys live there. Firstly,

Tiring and ungainly at first, perhaps, but impressive when mastered — army recruits learn the goose-step

Auld Lang Syne with visiting German pupils at Wanstead County High School in Essex, England. Before the war such exchanges were encouraged by Germany's leaders

the boys must be racially sound. Secondly, they must be physically fit – the standard of physical fitness is extraordinarily high. And thirdly, they must look reasonably honest (though their honesty is sometimes taken for granted if they have fair hair and blue eyes). In England we constantly hear the sportsman held up as a model type and an example to follow. In Germany it is the soldier: boys are taught to develop a soldierly attitude towards life.

'Games take up a very large part of the day's programme. There is no specialising. They are not out to produce record-breakers, but boys who have reached a reasonable degree of efficiency in a large number of games. The Germans demand roughly two things of a game: firstly, it must develop the muscles efficiently; and secondly, it must be a form of *Kampfsport* – that is to say, it must give ample scope for the fighting spirit . . . '

After the final year, in which each NAPOLA pupil sat his matriculation examination, labour service and service in one of the branches of the armed forces followed. It was then that the choice would have to be made of a career in the army, the party, the civil service, industry or academic life. Those who chose careers in areas other than the army then went on to take university courses which they were expected to complete with a PhD. The course of events did not allow this development and the first batches of graduates were immediately swallowed up by the army, where they soon created the impression of being excellent 'officer material'. Himmler's SS was not slow in making successful attempts at turning NAPOLAs into recruitment bases for

officers for the Waffen-SS, and with Himmler's growing influence new tendencies came to the fore which, prior to 1940, had not existed. Pupils in upper forms began to receive specifically anti-religious indoctrination by SS-officers from the SS-*Hauptamt* and these lessons ended regularly with veiled and sometimes more explicit invitations to the pupils to leave their respective religious denominations. Racial considerations in the selection became more specific. Doctors examining NAPOLA candidates were recruited inevitably from the SS and besides a thorough medical examination took skull measurements.

Older pupils of NAPOLAs in Germany's eastern regions were sent for short spells into German-occupied eastern European territories. On his return, each pupil had to submit a detailed report. One dating from August 1941 in Poland referred to the activities of a NAPOLA harvest team in the German annexed Warthegau.

Mastering the art of war weapons

Its author complained about the excessive reliance German 'settlers' had to place upon the availability of Polish labour which caused the Poles to drive the wage rates up. One 'settlement supervisor' received a favourable mention 'for teaching the Poles the

Rifle training at an Adolf Hitler School. The emphasis on para-military training rose appreciably when war broke out

only effective lesson with horsewhip and stick'. The introduction of greater mechanisation into farming methods was recommended which would reduce the dependence upon Polish labour. The police received severe reprimands for the neglect of its duties as did SS-building staff who hired Polish labour to build roads and bridges and then left them to themselves. According to the author of the report, the SS paid wages that were far too high and the Poles seemed to make the most of it by working correspondingly slowly. A visit to the Jewish ghetto at Lodz was also in the programme. The pupils 'were amused by the sight of the ghetto'.

One NAPOLA platoon leader who spent some time with his troops in Holland submitted an interesting report which throws light on the divisions within the camp of Dutch Nazi sympathisers. While they found cooperation between Germans and female members of the Dutch Labour Service good, that with the male Labour Service was much less so 'because it is led by anti-German Dutch officers whose removal even today causes some difficulty.' The Dutch youth movement of Mussert's NSB left a completely negative impression because of their 'moral laxity'. The NSB also lacked unity. Some of its leaders were in favour of a Greater Germanic Empire, others were primarily interested in Dutch independence. The Dutch SS told the NAPOLA pupils that as long as Dutch youth was with Mussert, it was completely in the wrong hands. The best thing that could happen was for Mussert to 'disappear altogether'. By comparison, the Dutch SS 'is ideologically unobjectionable and consciously orientated along the greater Germanic concept'. The German army however, appeared to enjoy a good reputation and its open band concerts were very well attended.

As the Allied bombing of Germany grew in intensity children were evacuated into less exposed areas, and grammar school pupils into *Kinderlandverschickungs* (KLV) homes, essentially camps in the countryside where teaching could continue uninterrupted. Those KLV camps close to a NAPOLA were immediately supervised politically by the Jungvolk and HJ leaders within the camps. This meant the introduction of a military discipline into the camps that was far more rigid than anything the ordinary Hitler Youth had been accustomed to. KLV camps who enjoyed this doubtful benefit thus became, for political purposes at least, NAPOLA extensions.

The emphasis upon para-military training rose appreciably during the last years of the war, the weapons chosen depending upon the pupils' physical capacity to handle them. At Bensberg for instance it was attempted to train eleven year olds to fire the short Italian carbine, Model 91, with the collapsible bayonet. But not only was the recoil too strong for the children, the samples of the weapon provided proved lethally defective. But an eleven year old could handle a 20mm anti-aircraft gun or a *Panzerfaust*. The members of the upper forms of that school actually manned the anti-aircraft guns around Cologne, while the younger ones were evacuated into the Eifel.

No order or decree was ever issued dissolving a NAPOLA in the face of the approaching Allies. Often the order was left in the hands of the head of the schools who was, however, reluctant to take the decision without the backing of a local party leader or an officer of the SS. But as the Allies advanced the future élite, in so far as it had not already been absorbed by the ranks of the Wehrmacht and SS, evaporated as quickly as it had been gathered.

Special formations

While within the NAPOLA the influence of the *Reichsjugendführung* was strictly circumscribed, it managed to extend its activities into other areas. This extension, however, was dictated by necessity. As critical Hitler Youth service reports about generally low standards within Hitler Youth units began to multiply, laxity in training and discipline were pointed to. No longer did the Hitler Youth represent a challenge; it had become just another part of the weekly routine. To counteract this and to induce new enthusiasm the Hitler Youth began to cater for the special interests of its members.

Gliding, of course, was the major sport, pioneered in Germany before 1933 and already in 1934 the German Airsport Association had begun to enrol schoolboys into its formations. Within the Hitler Youth, aviation enthusiasts formed themselves into groups, building model gliders. At the annual model gliding competition held in Germany in 1936 1,500 Hitler Youths participated. A year later for those over eighteen years of age the *NS-Flieger-Korps* was founded, which contained a body of trained gliding instructors as well as instructors for piston-engined aircraft. Shortly afterwards this was extended to the Hitler Youth by the foundation of the *Flieger*-HJ. Initially, the last two years of service with the *Jungvolk* were to serve as a preparatory stage for the *Flieger*-HJ, but by 1941 it had become the practice for aviation enthusiasts to serve as ten year olds, to pass two or three months in the Hitler Youth and then transfer to the *Flieger*-HJ.

What distinguished them from the general Hitler Youth was the airforce-blue uniform with light-blue piping, and the red-white-red armlet with swastika.

When in 1943 Hitler Youths were called up as *Luftwaffenhelfer* (Air Force Helpers) it did not affect the *Jungvolk*. However, in some parts of Germany, such as in Munich and Upper Bavaria, the order was interpreted to include the entire *Flieger*-HJ. The older ones manned the guns, the younger ones served in the communication network of the Flak, at searchlight batteries and as despatch riders. Only when, early in October 1943, a searchlight position manned entirely by eleven to fourteen year olds was knocked out by RAF raiders killing them all, was the initial order reformulated to exclude the younger age categories.

Basically the purpose of membership in the *Flieger*-HJ which reached a total of 78,000 was to acquire the rudimentaries of aviation knowledge, through building gliders first, acting as 'work horses' for the older ones who had to be catapulted up into the air for their first gliding test. Between the ages of fourteen and eighteen a member of the *Flieger*-HJ would try to obtain his A, B and C certificates in gliding. Another exciting aspect was the close contact that existed with the Luftwaffe at whose bases the *Flieger*-HJ recruits were frequent and welcome visitors, often being taken up in bombers or two-seater fighters.

Another special formation of the Hitler Youth was the *Motor*-HJ which, by 1933, had 3,000 members. The storm

Above: The craze of the thirties – gliding. This was one of the sports incorporated into the curriculum of the Hitler Youth. *Below:* Members of the special air force unit of the Hitler Youth – the *Flieger-HJ* – working with a glider

Above: Members of another special formation – the *Motor-HJ*. By 1933 this formation had some 3,000 members. *Below:* Future Graf von Spees? *Marine-HJ* recruits receive a cartography lesson

troopers had their own motorised branch, the *Nationalsozialistisches Kraftfahr Korps* (the NS Driving Corps), led by Major Huehnlein. In 1934 Huehnlein and Schirach agreed on co-operation and jointly formed the *Reichsmotorschule*. Every Hitler Youth could be a member from the age of sixteen onwards – the age when a German youth could officially obtain his first driving licence for a motor-cycle – and at the age of eighteen he would transfer to the NSKK. Membership figures diverge, for 1938 one source states that there were 90,000 recruits, another 102,000. In spite of this high number the *Motor*-HJ possessed only 300 motor cycles, the remainder were the private property of its members. In 1937 *Motor*-HJ members obtained 10,000 driving licences, a year later 28,000. But driving was only one part of the exercise, the other included a thorough mechanical knowledge, and a sound knowledge of the traffic code, both national and international. The ultimate purpose of this training is contained in an internal memorandum of the *Reichsjugendführung*: 'It is self-evident that members of the *Motor*-HJ will later serve in motorised units and in the driver corps of the Wehrmacht'. Consequently the demands made upon the members were high, besides all the other usual activities of the general Hitler Youth, a member of the *Motor*-HJ had to have annually a minimum of eighty hours driving and 105 hours service as a mechanic.

Very popular, particularly in northern Germany, was the *Marine*-HJ – the naval Hitler Youth – which reached a membership of 62,000 boys. In 1935 the first *Reichsseesportschule* was opened in Brandenburg, later followed by a second at the opposite end of Germany at Lake Constance. As in the case of the other special formations, so in the *Marine*-HJ demands made upon the individual boy both in terms of time and actual accomplishment were rather higher than those of the general Hitler Youth. Within its ranks, all the necessary sailing certificates could be obtained and before the war the most exciting experience was an exercise in the Baltic on one of the two sailing vessels used by the German navy for naval cadets, the *Gorch Fock* and the *Horst Wessel*. Other exercises included river navigation, as in 1940 when units of the *Marine*-HJ sailed in various vessels from Passau in Lower Bavaria, down the Danube, through Vienna and to Budapest. The conclusion of this exercise was a parade held by the *Marine*-HJ in Hungary's capital.

There were also smaller special formations, one of them a communications unit which in 1943 was absorbed by both the *Flieger*-HJ and the Air Force Helpers, another catered for future medics while yet another was the *Reiter*-HJ, a cavalry unit designed to attract mainly the youth of rural regions. When war broke out another special formation was created for air raid wardens, but such training as they received had by 1942 become part of the general training of every member of the *Jungvolk* and the HJ.

One kind of 'special service' required of every member of the Hitler Youth, male or female, irrespective of whether they belonged to special formations or not, was the land service. In a circular of 8th January 1940 it was explicitly stated, 'Land service is a political task of National Socialism. Its purpose is to bring back boys and girls from the cities to the land, to create new recruits for agricultural occupations and secure their continuity. The best of them should be given an opportunity to settle. The Hitler Youth is the sole executor of the land service . . .' In 1934 the first forty-five land service groups were founded and in 1939 11,752 boys and 14,264 girls helped to bring in the harvest. Because of lack of manpower during the war the total figure had increased to 38,522 in 1943 and by that time it was virtually impossible to distinguish between what was formally a 'land service group' and a Hitler Youth unit carrying out its land service in 'the battle of agricultural production'.

The dissenters

The HJ-*Streifendienst* had existed since 1934. Its primary function, in cooperation, if necessary, with the police and the Gestapo, was the supervision of Hitler Youth discipline, but its existence was also justified by the appearance of dissident factions within the Hitler Youth and without, and by the alarming rise of youth criminality after the outbreak of war.

Dissent had been voiced when the various leagues of the German youth movement had been dissolved before the summer of 1933. Former youth leaders, even if they joined the Hitler Youth, were always politically suspect. Friedrich Hielscher, a man of some prominence in the opposition to Hitler, put his youth group under the protection of the SS. He had told his members: 'We must be fully in the picture about what is going on. We have to have a man who will cover us.' Others, the most prominent being Otto Strasser's 'Black Front', entered Robert Ley's KDF, 'Strength through Joy' movement. During the early phase of Hitler's régime it was still possible to transfer to one of the new movements but as he consolidated his position, the question of just how far National Socialism could be combatted from within, how far tactical cooperation on the surface could continue without putting at stake fundamental issues of principle and involving individual participation in Nazi crimes, could no longer be ignored.

On Schirach's initiative a round-up of the leaders of the German youth movements began. Some regained their liberty but remained under Gestapo surveillance, others were liquidated in the course of the June purge of 1934. Adalbert Probst, one of the leaders of the Catholic Youth movement, was killed 'while trying to escape arrest' and the same fate met another youth leader, Plauen Karl Laemmermann. At the same time Schirach began to purge the upper echelons of the Hitler Youth leadership of formerly prominent members of other youth movements. Some managed to escape and emigrate, but lost their German citizenship in consequence. Others spent years in concentration camps such as Dachau, where many of them perished. The bulk of those who emigrated chose as their residence countries directly adjoining Germany where they could keep in touch with developments at home and try to influence them. The greatest activity emanated from Czechoslovakia where, in Eger and Prague, former youth movement leaders continued publishing their periodicals and propaganda leaflets which were then smuggled into Germany. Austria proved a disappointment because first Dollfuss and then Schuschnigg clamped down on the illegal activities of German emigrants.

Though deprived of leaders, formations within the Hitler Youth or German Youth movement caused concern to Schirach until the outbreak of war. Nor did he always find an ally in the German judiciary if a former youth

Above left: Otto Strasser, leader of the 'Black Front'. *Above right:* Adalbert Probst, one of the Catholic Youth leaders, shot by the Gestapo. *Below:* The gateway to death? A concentration camp near Berlin. Such camps existed long before the war to take care of 'dissident elements' in German society

leader was caught and put on trial for violating paragraph 4 of the decree of the *Reichspresident* for protection of People and State.

Decrees dissolving the existing youth organisations had to be repeated time and again and in order to obtain another lever against the leaders of 'illegal' youth movements, sexual offences, especially homosexuality, were often alleged. The German Youth Movement was virtually destroyed. Its continued illegal existence could only be carried on at a very restricted local level, and even there agents of *HJ-Streifendienst* managed to infiltrate. Hesse, Hanover, Dessau, Hamburg and Berlin were, relatively speaking, strongholds of illegal youth movements. In southern Germany they seem to have played a less prominent role, at least the police records have not much to report about them, but several members of the opposition group *Weisse Rose*, (White Rose) came from illegal youth groups.

Among the former youth organisations of the political parties of the left and of the trade unions a remarkable transformation took place. Ideological barriers were broken and a youth group such as the Red Assault Troop founded by Rudolf Kuestermeier included Socialists, Communists, Democrats, Catholics and Protestants. Its centre was in Berlin with branches in most major German cities but by late 1934 they had all become victims of the Gestapo. Others continued but, even if they were not caught, remained politically insignificant.

Theoretically, the denominational youth groups had a longer span of survival than any of the others. In practice the protestant youth movement had been eroded from without and within, while, at least for the time being, the Concordat allowed the continued existence of Catholic Youth groups. Even after Hitler Youth service had become compulsory according to the law, it was still possible also to be a member of the Catholic Youth, in spite of Schirach's assertion to the contrary. Court cases on this issue were usually decided in favour of the accused. But there were also other means of harrassment. Catholic Youth literature was confiscated, Catholic civil servants were threatened with dismissal if their children would not leave the Catholic Youth and become members of the Hitler Youth. Public appearances of closed formations of uniformed Catholic Youths groups were forbidden and this included summer camps. Nevertheless, at Easter 1935 Catholic Youths numbering 2,000 made a pilgrimage to Rome where they were personally received by Pope Pius XI. From 1937 onwards, when the Hitler Youth had become the 'state youth organisation', measures against them toughened, and their leaders were put on trial. Only in March 1939 were denominational youth organisations formally forbidden, denominational youth activity was to be restricted exclusively to the respective parish. This did not mean the end of harassment; raids by local Hitler Youth groups were frequent and meetings had to be held in secret. In Munich, for instance, at night in the cellar of the municipal electricity administration, or in the midst of one of its largest cemetaries, the *Waldfriedhof*.

The outbreak of war again posed a question of conscience. No detailed study of how this was answered is available, but for most, now that the country was at war, their duty was to the Fatherland. To quote again an example with which the author is familiar, late in October 1939 various members of Catholic Youth groups in Munich met at the Franciscan Monastery of St Anna in the heart of Munich and formally dissolved their groups until war's end.

Quite another kind of opposition which the Hitler Youth faced in increasing numbers after 1936 was that by gangs of hostile youths. They were not necessarily members of former youth movements; their common denominator, if indeed they had one, was the rejection of compulsory Hitler Youth service. Mostly they were perforce Hitler Youth members already. But they teamed up to disrupt local Hitler Youth meetings and to attack Hitler Youth leaders. They established their centres in the large cities, most prominently in the industrial area of the Ruhr, and harboured criminal elements.

The first official body to mete out punishment to these youths was the Hitler Youth itself which, since March 1940, had also acquired certain judiciary rights. It could issue formal warnings, reprimands, promotion witdrawal, degredation, arrest (to be executed at weekends with a diet of bread and water) but only to youths up to the age of fourteen. For 1942 this last disciplinary measure was carried out in sixty-five per cent of the cases for violations against private property, ten per cent for sexual offences and the remainder for 'school offences', mainly for playing truant. Generally the highest quota of juvenile delinquency during the war came from the blacked-out cities of western and central Germany.

For gangs to form within the Hitler Youth was not unknown although there is no evidence pointing to ideological and idealistic anti-Nazi motivation. If not criminal, the motivation was such as makes many youths anywhere rebel against conformity and, as in Hitler's Germany, against compulsory regimentation.

Members of one youthful opposition group which was to enter and leave the scene tragically were by the time of their action already soldiers. Hans Scholl, born in 1918 in Ulm studied medicine, his sister Sophie biology and philosophy. Hans Scholl had seen action in Russia and was given special leave to continue his medical studies at the University of Munich where his sister was also a student. Before 1936 he had been an enthusiastic member of the *Jungvolk* in which he reached the rank of *Fahnleinsführer* but subsequent events,

Hans Scholl, martyr to his belief that Hitler was wrong

Sophie Scholl, sister of Hans and likewise an agitator for the fall of Hitler's regime. Both brother and sister were decapitated by the Gestapo

141

Roland Freisler, President of the 'People's Court' and one of the official voices of Nazi persecution

Paul Giesler, *Gauleiter* for Munich and Upper Bavaria. He favoured repressive measures against Munich students in order to 'heighten their morale'

and the anti-Catholic policy of the Hitler Youth, robbed him of his illusions and reactivated his interest in the Catholic Youth. The Scholls were joined in Munich by another former member of the Catholic Youth, Willi Graf. He too studied medicine. They were joined by two other students, Alexander Schmorell and Christoph Probst. They met regularly at the flat of Professor Kurt Huber, another member of the group that eventually called itself the 'White Rose'.

Towards the end of 1942 the *Gauleiter* for Munich and Upper Bavaria, Paul Giesler, had addressed Munich's students and expressed his opinion of the low standard of their morale. His speech was badly received and he was frequently interrupted. The Scholls and their friends exploited the dissatisfaction among the students and agitated against a régime which in their opinion had lost any moral right to continue to lead Germany. If it remained, they believed it would lead Germany into disaster the spectre of which could already be seen in North Africa and even more impressive and psychologically oppressive at Stalingrad.

Less than a fortnight after its fall, on the morning of 16th February 1943, citizens of Munich who were walking towards the *Siegestor*, the arch of victory, saw inscriptions painted on the wall calling for 'Freedom' and 'Down with Hitler'. Russian women were ordered to scrub off the inscriptions further up the street where they appeared again on the wall of the university. During the two preceeding months many of Munich's citizens had already been alarmed by finding in their letter boxes duplicated leaflets calling for an end to the Nazi regime, and encouraging the German people to rid themselves by their own efforts of a government which, in the name of the German people, had perpetrated crimes so immense that even those who heard of them refused to believe until finally confronted with them.

Two days after the 'slogan painting

action', on Thursday, 18th February, Hans and Sophie Scholl started another leaflet action, this time inside the university. Early in the morning before lectures began they distributed handouts in the lecture halls and when some were left they emptied the suit case from the top floor of the main hall of the university, scattering them in the entrance hall. The university caretaker saw them and immediately called the police. All exits of the university were closed, the police arrived and took the Scholls to the *Wittelsbach Palais*, now the Gestapo headquarters. Their flat was searched and this search revealed the names of the other members of the 'White Rose'. Roland Freisler, the notorious president of the 'People's Court' arrived in Munich and the trial was held on 22nd February. Christoph Probst was also accused. The trial was brief and the sentence was death by decapitation. On the afternoon of the same day the condemned were allowed to see their closest relatives for the last time. Sophie was the first to die 'free, fearless and relaxed with a smile on her face'. Hans Scholl, before putting his head on the block, shouted so that it resounded throughout the prison 'Long live liberty'. Probst followed.

Schmorell, Willi Graf and Professor Huber were arrested a few weeks later and the sentence of death was carried out on them on 13th August 1943 at the prison of Munich, Stadelheim, the same prison where Röhm and many of his associates had met their fate. Their death was in vain, the hope that it would cause repercussions throughout Germany proved futile. Their memory was to be resurrected by a guilt-ridden generation, a kind of atonement, but they did not change the course of events. Nor did any of the other young Germans who tried to take the initiative; their warnings and exortations evaporated in a vacuum, and yet they were the youth who had changed the words of an old song of the German Youth movement to say –
We are criminals in your state
And are proud of our crime.
We are the youth of high treason
And shall break this servitude.
Between 1940 and 1945 in the prison of Brandenburg alone 1,807 inmates were executed for political reasons. Seventy-five of them were under twenty years old, twenty-two were pupils and students, one had just reached the age of sixteen. Of all Germans sentenced for political reasons in Hamburg between 1933 and 1945, eleven per cent were youths. The will to resist was there in some, too few, but it was there all the same and the supreme price was paid.

In the Second World War

The outbreak of war saw the Hitler Youth prepared; the invocation of the myth of Langemarck had done its service and would continue doing it for the next six years. As one of the leading functionaries of the *Reichsjugendführung* wrote: '. . . From the experience of the World War was born the idea of National Socialism, out of its armies came the unknown frontline soldier, Adolf Hitler, as its leader. The myth of the sacrifice in the World War of Germany's youth has given to the postwar youth a new faith and a new strength to unfold the ideals of National Socialism. Since all education, according to the maxims of the *Reichsjugendführer* rests on the examples provided, so it was explicable that the German youth in the war as well as Herbert Norkus and others later gave their lives for a new Germany and that this sacrifice was the most decisive precondition for a revolutionary educational idea and its youth movement.'

The *Reichsjugendführer*, Baldur von Schirach, however, received preferential treatment. Drafted into the army towards the end of 1939, within less than six months he completed his career from simple recruit to full lieutenant. His military career ended on 2nd August 1940 when he was appointed *Gauleiter* of Vienna. In his place, Arthur Axman, who had just lost an arm, was appointed as *Reichsjugendführer*. He proved to be a reliable and efficient organiser who commanded the respect of his subordinates.

The government immediately put to full use the readily available enthusiasm among the Hitler Youth. Throughout the war incidents occurred time and again of a member of the *Jungvolk* faking his birth certificate by a year or two to be accepted, because father or brother had been called up and they too 'wanted to do their bit'. They were usually allowed to stay.

Arthur Axmann, who replaced Baldur von Schirach as *Reichsjugendführer*

During the Polish campaign in Germany's eastern provinces schools were cleared and turned into army quarters and Hitler youths served as couriers. The upper echelons of the Hitler Youth shrank perceptably. On 1st October 1939 of 424 male Hitler Youth leaders who belonged to the *Reichsjugendführung* 273 served in the *Wehrmacht*. Of 1,100 *Bann* and *Jungbannführers* 467 were in the armed forces, of the 10,572 fatal casualties of the Polish campaign 314 had been Hitler Youth Leaders of the upper ranks.

Special tasks were now delegated to the *Jungvolk* and to the HJ and the female equivalents. Once a month they distributed ration cards to each household, they collected scrap metal, clothes, skis – anything that was asked for and almost always got it. If it was refused they 'organised' it, a term soon to become a synonym for stealing. Girl groups were despatched to field hospitals to entertain and care for the wounded, they helped in state kindergartens, and provided troop trains in transit with drink and food. Between party offices Hitler Youths established a regular messenger service which was later extended to the offices and barracks of the armed forces inside Germany. Participation in agricultural work was increased. In 1940 alone members of the BDM assisted in 318,782 households, 64,106 in the Red Cross, 60,263 in army hospitals and 107,185 at railway stations. For them 'total war' came at a considerably earlier stage than for the rest of Germany's civilian population.

From October 1939 para-military training of the Hitler Youth was intensified and carried out every weekend, led by a former Hitler Youth leader who had also obtained the Knight's Cross. The delegation of frontline officers to units of the *Jungvolk* and HJ became a permanent feature from 1940 onwards. All this led to a reduction of the amount of 'political instruction'. With the extension of

145

Hitler Youth girls distribute ration cards as one of their tasks

Germany's power, especially in the east, special Hitler Youth units were despatched to Poland and other eastern European regions to organise the Hitler Youth among the 'racial Germans', an undertaking of some difficulty when, as in many cases, the 'Germans' could speak no German at all. Furthermore, after 1941 when the Greater Germanic Empire gained a short-lived currency, the Hitler Youth, in cooperation with the SS, assembled 'Eastern volunteers of the Germanic Youth' – German, Dutch, Belgian, Danish and Norwegian youths who, after intensive training courses, acted in supervisory functions on the farm collectives of Russia and the Ukraine. This endeavour to combine the fascist youth organisations of German-occupied or German-dominated parts of Europe culminated in September 1942 when Axmann and Schirach jointly convened a European Youth Meeting and created the 'European Youth League'. Members of the League included Italy's Fascist Youth Movement, the Youth Movement of the Spanish Falange, the Flemish National Socialist Youth, the Walloon Rexist Youth, the Bulgarian Brannik-Youth, the Danish and Dutch National Socialist Youth, the Finnish Youth Movement, the Croat Ustashi Youth, the Norwegian Nasjonal-Samling-Youth, the Rumanian State Youth, the Slovak Hlinka Youth and the Hungarian Levante Youth. Japanese Youth leaders were also present as guests.

As in the prewar years, each of the war years, with the exception of 1945, was headed by a particular slogan for the Hitler Youth; 1940 was 'The Year of Testing', 1941 was 'Our Life as a Road to the Führer', 1942 was 'Youth in the East and on the Land', 1943 'War

Special Hitler Youth units were dispatched to eastern Europe to organize young 'Racial Germans'

The poet Gottfried Benn, who characterized Hitler Youth education as: 'the elimination of the intellectual and moral content of literature'

Action of the German Youth' and 1944 the 'Year of War Volunteers'. Those who had joined the Hitler Youth before or in the early 1930s were by 1941 veteran soldiers, those who followed them were determined to meet Hitler's demand for youth 'fast like greyhounds, tough like leather and hard like Krupp steel'. Special camps for para-military training were established, the *Wehrertüchtigungslager*, in which members of the HJ were given basic infantry training. The German expressionist poet and lyricist, Gottfried Benn, who was by profession an army doctor, noted as late as 1944 'The German army is carried essentially by two commissioned ranks, the morbid Field-Marshals forever listening to Hitler, and the young lieutenants. The lieutenants emerged from the Hitler Youth and therefore have an education behind them the essence of which was the elimination of the intellectual and moral content of literature, replaced by Gothic princes, daggers – and for whom marching exercises, bedding down in hay lofts, became a way of life. They were already in peace time far removed from those still educated in

the old traditions, from parents, educators, clergymen and humanistic circles. With their aim before them they are well equipped for the task of deliberately destroying part of the globe in the name of the Aryan mission.'

Basic training became shorter and shorter. From January 1943 onwards most anti-aircraft batteries were manned by Hitler Youths, so were searchlight batteries, and communication networks. Members of the *Jungvolk* acted as despatch riders. After the raids it was up to the older men of the party organisations and the Hitler Youths to rehouse those who had been bombed out. Many a Hitler Youth made himself a bad name locally for successfully ferreting out large flats occupied by one single owner who, only with reluctance and police enforcement, would open his or her doors to those who had lost their homes. As the bombing offensive increased in intensity boys and girls who were really mere children spent days and nights just dishing out meals to the victims, and guarding their salvaged property, usually stacked under the open sky, against looters.

Sometimes war service could come unexpectedly out of the blue, like to the *Flieger*-HJ unit from Munich (whose ages ranged from ten to fifteen) which in July 1944 was in Pomerania for a gliding holiday. Suddenly they received orders to proceed to Allenstein in East Prussia and from there to Bischofsburg. Nearby the local population was digging anti-tank ditches. The older ones were detailed for that work, the younger ones for less strenuous work. One member of this group remembered: 'We put up our tents and cooked some macaroni while the sun cast its last rays across the fields. Too tired to sing we went to sleep.

'In the middle of the night I woke up,

Berlin, 1945. One of the Hitler Youth dispatch riders who kept communications open in the besieged city

Above: Ten-year-old HJ members help to salvage property and guard it against looters. *Below:* Hitler Youths dig trenches

scared out of my sleep by a distant rumbling. I pushed Gerd who slept next to me. "What is the matter?" he asked dozily. "Can you hear the rumbling?"

"What rumbling?"

"Listen!" It sounded like an endless column of heavy lorries driving across a steel bridge. We crawled out of our tents. The night was cool and the dew glistened dimly in the calm light of the moon. Our guard sat wrapped in blankets beside the fire. He was awake.

"Can you see it?" he asked.

'In the east the horizon formed a long red line, broken at intervals by fireflashes. In parts the line became feeble for seconds and at times extinguished completely. Minutes later, the flashes which actually caused this red line returned and so restored its continuity.

"I hope it never gets as far as down here" said Gerd. "My father is in Russia and he said if they should ever get into Germany we should kill ourselves, for what we could expect from the Russians would be even worse."

"Oh, they will never get so far, we will beat them to the devil. All the same I should be glad if we get back soon," I said.

"I hope so too" said our guard, who was a boy from the second platoon. "My mother will give me a mighty good thrashing. She will never believe me when I tell her that they had sent us to dig trenches." '

With the growing influence of the SS in the Hitler Youth during the war years, the recruitment drives of the Waffen-SS were concentrated on the HJ, and under the impact of 'total war' in 1943 the idea occurred to create a special division of the Hitler Youth within the Waffen-SS, which ultimately was to be the 12th SS-Panzer division Hitlerjugend. Goebbels objected on the grounds that it might provide the enemy propaganda with ammunition. But, overruled by Hitler, in June 1943 the order was issued to set up the division.

In the main the recruits were to be drawn from the Hitler Youth's special camps for para-military training while the nucleus of experienced officers and NCOs was to be drawn from Hitler's former bodyguard, the Leibstandarte SS Adolf Hitler. This proved a not altogether satisfactory measure. The LSAH had suffered heavy losses in the recapture of Charcov in February/March 1943 and was itself in the process of refitting and training replacements in order to play a vital role in the projected Kursk offensive.

The 12th SS Panzer-Division's most serious shortage was in experienced company, platoon and squad leaders. It was a step dictated by expediency to promote platoon commanders rapidly to company commanders. Another alternative chosen was the drafting of army officers who previously had been Hitler Youth leaders into the Hitler Youth Division to fill the vacancies. To obtain the necessary squad or section leaders Hitler Youths who in the special camps had shown a 'special aptitude for military leadership' were, after their initial basic training, sent to the Waffen-SS NCO school at Lauenburg and within three months trained to be NCOs. They lacked the reality of battle experience as much as those whom they were to lead into battle.

SS-Standartenführer Fritz Whitt, a battle-hardened officer decorated with the Knight's Cross and Oakleaves, was appointed as the first commander of the Hitler Youth Division.

During July and August 1943 the first batches of recruits arrived, a total of approximately 10,000 boys, many of whom were not quite seventeen years old. Nor were they all volunteers. Many had previously volunteered for other branches of the armed services such as the Luftwaffe but when they were called up found themselves unexpectedly in Waffen-SS barracks. Others had been talked into volunteering, but able leadership soon managed to overcome initial misgivings and infused an aggressive enthusiasm

Above: SS troops. Goebbels objected to a special SS division, the 12th SS-Panzer Division *Hitlerjugend,* being formed. *Below left:* SS-*Standartenführer* Fritz Witt, who was appointed the first commander of the Hitler Youth Division. *Below right:* Heinz Guderian, who was impressed by the enthusiasm of the Hitler Youth Division

which was not found wanting when put to the real test in Normandy a year later.

The beginnings were hardly auspicious; when the boys arrived at their training garrison at Beverloo in Belgium there were not even enough uniforms for them. Nevertheless, basic training began almost immediately. By the end of September 1943 these shortcomings had been overcome and the division had been organised in all its essential components. A month later it was transformed into a Panzer-Division, though conspicuously lacking in armour. The Panzer regiment which was being formed near Reims had only four Panzer Mark IV and four Panthers. Even these had been brought back 'unofficially' from the Eastern Front. The artillery regiment had only a few light howitzers while cars, lorries and traction vehicles were almost non-existent. As a first measure the Hitler Youth Division received vehicles requisitioned from the Italian army, now split into pro-Allied and a smaller pro-German contingent. During December 1943 and the early months of 1944 armour began to be more plentiful. When Generaloberst Guderian visited one of the first field exercises of the Hitler Youth Division he was impressed by both the enthusiasm of the boys and high degree of efficiency reached in so short a time.

By comparison with other *Waffen*-SS or *Wehrmacht* units, the Hitler Youth Division knew no 'square bashing' or goose-stepping exercising. Given the youth of the recruits it was rightly assumed that such forms of training would only undermine their morale and great emphasis was put upon informal relationship between officers and men and a divisional order asked all company commanders to take up contact with the parents of the recruits. The emphasis in training was placed upon actual combat carried out under actual combat conditions, supplemented by sports exercises. Upon Guderian's suggestion no target practice took place in barrack training grounds but in the actual field and the lessons learnt from the Russian infantry and armour as regards the importance of effective camouflage were driven home to the boys.

Because of their age, the boys received special rations and up to the age of eighteen received a sweet ration in lieu of cigarettes – a regulation very much resented by those affected.

On 6th June 1944 the division moved into battle, but already on its seventy-mile march from its base to the Caen sector it had been heavily mauled by the strafing attacks by Allied fighter bombers. But in their first attack they knocked out twenty-eight Canadian tanks at the loss of only six of their own. They fought the rest of the Normandy campaign in this area and as Chester Wilmot records 'The troops of the 12th SS, who were holding this sector, fought with a tenacity and ferocity seldom equalled and never excelled during the whole campaign'. They sprang at Allied tanks 'like wolves' as a British tank commander said, 'until we were forced to kill them against our will'.

On 16th June 1944 the Divisional Commander Witt was killed and replaced by Kurt Meyer, *Panzermeyer*, at the age of thirty-three the youngest divisional commander in the German army. The son of a worker, himself an ex-miner, police officer and then one of the early members of the SS-*Verfuegungstruppe*, he typified the 'political soldier' but he possessed great gifts of personal leadership and was a good tactician. Frequently described as an 'unrepentant Nazi fanatic', it ought to be added that it was primarily due to his influence in the late 1950s and early 1960s before his death, that the *Waffen*-SS's exservicemen's organisation broke such ties as existed with Neo-Nazi organisations and became a body dominated by political moderates.

Normandy was not only the testing ground of the Hitler Youth Division, it was also its grave. By 4th September 1944 when it crossed the Meuse near Yvoir the Division consisted of 600 men, without tanks, and without ammunition for the artillery. 'It is a pity that this faithful youth is sacrificed in a hopeless situation' commented Field Marshal von Rundstedt.

After Normandy the Hitler Youth Division continued to exist in name, but its recruits were like those of most other German divisions scraped from the barrel of Germany's manpower reserves. At home with the creation of the *Volkssturm* in October 1944 officially every male from sixteen to sixty was subject to military service, in practice the new 'recruits' were often much younger as well as older. After all, even eleven year-olds could fire a recoilless *Panzerfaust*. Even girls, incapable of loading a machine gun or Luger pistol, 'manned' anti-aircraft batteries as in the 6th battery of the Flak Reserve unit 61 at Vienna-Kagran. During a daylight raid on Vienna one of their 88mm guns shot down a Liberator bomber; shortly afterwards it received a direct hit which killed three girls and wounded two.

To the last moment Germany's youth was exhorted to mount and assist the defence of the Reich against the 'Bolshevik hordes' and the 'Anglo-American gangsters'. Many of them followed the call and perished, Hitler Youths helped to defend Hitler's bunker and one of the last decorations awarded by Hitler was to the twelve year-old Alfred Czech who received the Iron Cross, 2nd class. The boys of the Hitler Youth Division had received sound training, those who followed were simply thrown into the furnace of war with no other preparation than the myth of Langemarck and the legends of 'the heroes of the National Socialist movement'.

One such group of frightened little boys manned the barricade erected from street-cars across Munich's Maximilian bridge. The youngest was about ten, the oldest not quite fourteen years old. Equipped with Panzerfausts, they were too frightened to fire them against a seemingly endless col-

eft: Kurt Meyer, commander of 12th SS-Division. An ex-miner, he was the oungest divisional commander in the Germany army. *Below:* Volkssturm ecruits, the German equivalent of the Home Guard. *Above:* Hitler Youth and 'olkssturm trenches together in defence of the Fatherland

Above: Boys of the Hitler Youth Division, thrown into war with little other preparation than myths and legends. *Below:* A GI guards captured boy soldiers of the Hitler Youth. *Right:* Hitler Youth members in captivity. At the age of eleven or twelve, their world has collapsed

umn of Shermans that rumbled down Munich's Maximilianstrasse. It was Monday, 30th April 1945. At about the same time that their Führer committed suicide these Hitler Youths were taken prisoners of war. The following day they were taken to a place of which they had so far heard only in disbelieving whispers: to the liberated concentration camp at Dachau.

'To our left and right soldiers mingled with concentration camp inmates, the latter wearing the vertically blue and white striped suits which hung on figures so thin, it was impossible to believe that these people could still speak, let alone walk. Their heads were either shaven or otherwise covered by a beret of the same material as the suits. The gate was flanked by two Sherman tanks, its crews sitting on turret and hulls feeding the surrounding men with chewing gum and chocolate. . . . During the first few moments after entering the compound, I thought the former inmates were going to tear us to pieces. Astonishingly enough, they just flanked the way wherever we went, but never a word was uttered, not a hand raised against us. First we were taken to a railway siding that branched off from the SS main camp. We were ordered to halt before a number of trucks. An American soldier fetched a few of us out (apparently the strongest looking ones) and in perfect German ordered us to open one of these freight trucks. With crow bars and a good deal of strength we pushed back the doors.

'The first thing that fell out was the skeleton of a woman. After that nothing more fell out, for dead bodies were standing so close to each other, like sardines, that one supported the other . . . The next thing we were taken to was a red brick building enveloped by an acrid smell. We entered a hall and, for a moment, we thought we were in a boiler room with a number of big stoves. That idea was immediately dispelled when we saw before each stove a stretcher made of metal with iron clamps. Some of these stretchers

were still halfway in the stove covered by the remnants of burnt bodies. That night was a sleepless one. The impact of what we had seen was too great to be immediately digested. I could not help but cry.'

For this Hitler Youth already at the age of eleven a world had collapsed. He was but one of millions. Little more than a month after this gruesome spectacle was revealed to children, the 'poet' of the Hitler Youth anthem and its former leader, Baldur von Schirach handed himself over to the Allies

subsequently to disappear for twenty years behind the walls of the Fortress of Spandau.

Now and again one thinks back to the boys and girls, as the case may be, thrown together by crisis, by stark naked fear and by the belief in their country. One cherishes the sense of comradeship of the past and is tempted to look with contempt upon those excluded from that close community, from that spirit of comradeship for which, in an industrial competitive society, there is little or no room. But

Adolf Hitler offered youthful idealists a cause for self-sacrifice. A few days before his death, he decorates a member of the Hitler Youth

that temptation towards nostalgia disappears as quickly as it comes, for with it appear the memories of the victims, of the innocent, of the appalling misuse made of the idealism and the willingness for personal sacrifice; they were worthy of a better cause than that which their Führer had to offer.

Bibliography

Der Mythos vom III Reich by J F Neurohr (Stuttgart)
Elite für die Diktatur by H Neberhorst (Düsseldorf)
Führung und Verführung by H J Gamm (Munich)
Gewalt und Gewissen edited by K Vielhaber (Frankfurt)
Hitlerjugend by A Klönne (Frankfurt)
Ich glaubte an Hitler by Baldur von Schirach (Hamburg)
The Face of the Third Reich by J C Fest (London)
The German Dictatorship by K D Bracher (London)